SALT TIDE

SALT TIDE

Cycles and Currents
of Life along the Coast

Curtis J. Badger

THE
COUNTRYMAN
PRESS

Library of Congress Cataloging-in-Publication Data

Badger, Curtis J.
  Salt tide : cycles and currents of life along the coast / Curtis J. Badger. — 1st pbk. ed.
            p.   cm.
  Originally published: Harrisburg, PA : Stackpole Books, © 1993.
  Includes bibliographical references.
  ISBN 0-88150-463-7 (pbk.)
  1. Island animals—Virginia. 2. Island plants—Virginia.
3. Barrier islands—Virginia. 4. Natural history—Virginia.
I. Title
  [QH105.V8B33 1999]
  508.755'1—dc21   98-53509
                                                        CIP

Cover design by Mark Olszewski
Cover illustration and interior art by Harry Jaecks
Map by Donna Ziegenfuss

Published by The Countryman Press
PO Box 748, Woodstock, VT 05091

Distributed by W. W. Norton & Company, Inc.
500 Fifth Avenue, New York, NY 10110

Printed in the United States of America

10 9 8 7 6 5 4 3 2 1

To Tom,
who understood from the beginning

Come, dear children, let us away;
    Down and away below.
Now my brothers call from the bay;
Now the great winds shoreward blow;
Now the salt tides seaward flow;
Now the wild white horses play,
Champ and chafe and toss in the spray.
Children dear, let us away,
This way, this way.

From "The Forsaken Merman"
Matthew Arnold, 1822–1888

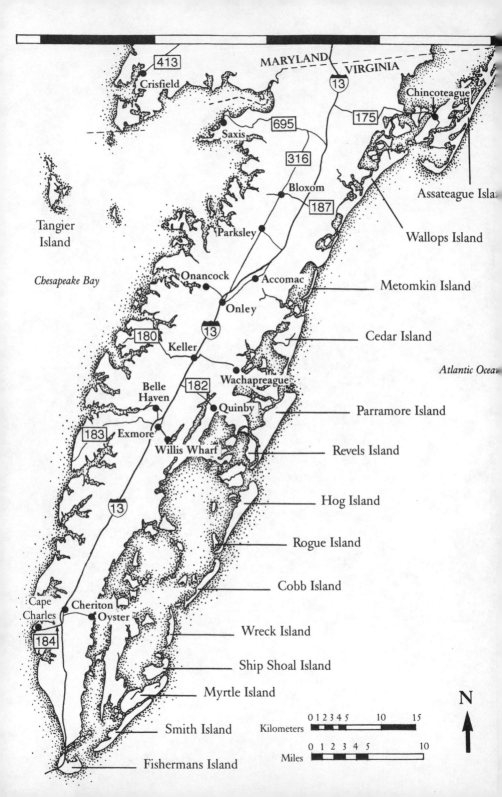

Contents

**Introduction:
The Last of the Silence**
1

Clam Sign
9

Spartina
19

Flounder Season
33

Life at the Edge
41

Plover Watch
51

CONTENTS

Beachcombing
61

Small Boats
73

Salted Fish
83

Teal
89

December Light
93

The Henning Tides
103

Captain John's Treasure
113

Genetic Navigation
123

Bibliography
131

Acknowledgments

I would like to thank first of all my wife, Lynn, and son, Tom, whose enthusiasm for salt marshes, barrier beaches, and tidal creeks heightens my own pleasure and awareness.

I would like to thank The Nature Conservancy for protecting these special places through creation of the Virginia Coast Reserve. And to John Hall, director of the Virginia Coast Reserve, special thanks for allowing me to roam at will over the islands, marshes, and mainland farms.

I am not a scientist, so I am indebted to those who are for their guidance in the more technical sections of the book. Mike Castagna and Gene Silberhorn of the Virginia Institute of Marine Science provided much helpful information on clams and salt marsh plants. John Hall and John Terres provided general guidance and suggestions.

Many thanks to Judith Schnell, my editor, for her encouragement, good counsel, and editing skills.

And most of all I would like to thank my dad, who taught me to love the places described here. I miss our fishing trips and beach walks, and I wish he were still here so I might thank him personally. Although he is no longer with us, I feel, somehow, that he can sense my gratitude.

Introduction:
The Last
of the Silence

This is a book about the barrier islands and salt marshes of the Virginia coast, but the descriptions of plants and animals apply to most of the islands and salt marshes that line the unglaciated Atlantic coast, from the south shore of Long Island to Florida. The coastal barrier beaches are typically long, low, narrow, sandy islands separated from one another by narrow inlets and from the mainland by shallow bays, winding creeks, vast salt marshes, and tidal flats.

It is a wonderfully productive system. Not only do the islands protect the mainland from storms, but also the marshes and shallow bays provide homes for many species of fish, shellfish, mollusks, migrating waterfowl, and shorebirds. Acre for acre, the salt marsh is one of the most productive natural systems on earth; it is a giant protein factory that supports a wide variety of life, ranging from microscopic zooplankton to those of us at the top of the food chain.

Because of their remoteness and inaccessibility, the islands along the east coast of the United States attracted little attention until shortly after the Civil War. Then, with rail transportation making travel along the coast downright luxurious, many of our coastal islands became havens for summer vacationers and autumn waterfowl hunters. With the advent of the motorcar early in this century, bridges were built to link islands to mainland roads and to one another. Soon the demand for island property grew, and development began in earnest. As a result, the wild beaches found by seventeenth-century European colonists are now, for the most part, extensively developed, and many of the vast marshes that lay between the beaches and mainland have been converted to homesites, recreation areas, farmland, and even industrial parks and landfills.

The extraordinary thing about the Virginia islands and salt marshes is that they are today much as they were three centuries ago. Eighteen separate islands buffer the Virginia coast, covering some one hundred miles, from Sinepuxent Bay at the northern tip of Assateague Island in Maryland to Smith and Fisherman islands at the entrance to Chesapeake Bay. The islands are protected through a cooperative arrangement among the federal government, which owns four islands; the state of Virginia, owner of one barrier island and one interior island; and the Nature Conservancy, a private land conservation organization that began assembling its Virginia Coast Reserve in the early 1970s, when a group of investors planned a large development on the three southernmost islands. After buying out the investors, the Conservancy added to its holdings, which now include more than forty thousand acres on thirteen islands, vast marshes, and several mainland farms on the seaside watershed.

INTRODUCTION

Although there are numerous wildlife refuges and protected seashores elsewhere along the coast, the Virginia islands form the last intact, unspoiled barrier island ecosystem on the coast. Other than at the National Wildlife Refuge on Assateague Island and the NASA launch facility on Wallops Island, there are no roads, no hotels—none of the reminders that we have lost most of the wilderness that once lined the east coast of the United States. On these islands, you can walk for hours and see only gulls and shorebirds, sand dunes and breaking surf and endless ocean. The island system is large enough, and remote enough, to be considered a true coastal wilderness, the last one we have on the Atlantic, providing the same gifts to humans as do the mountain ranges and canyonlands of the West, even if these islands are somewhat more hemmed in by civilization.

The important thing about wilderness, any wilderness, is the effect it has on the human spirit. Hiking a wilderness beach is different from hiking a resort beach, or even a national seashore beach where development is held to a minimum. It has to do, I think, with the great value of seclusion, with places that are wild and remote and provide the illusion, if only for a few hours or a few days, of being untouched. A wilderness beach is defiled by a modest two-lane highway because the road destroys the illusion of remoteness. A single house on a remote island or on a salt marsh defiles it for similar reasons; it reminds us of the some-times stifling nearness of civilization.

We need barrier island wildernesses for the same reasons we need wildernesses in the mountains, canyons, or deserts of the Southwest. In the words of Wallace Stegner, "Wilderness has helped form our character and has shaped our history as a people. . . . Something will have gone out of us as a people if we ever let the remaining wilderness be destroyed; if we permit the last virgin forests to be turned into comic books and plastic

cigarette cases . . . and push our paved roads through the last of the silence, so that never again will Americans be free in their own country from the noise, the exhausts, the stinks of human and automotive waste."

When it comes to America's coast, precious little silence remains; we have pushed our paved roads through the best of it. Saving wilderness, after all, is an undemocratic process, one that runs counter to our tradition of equal rights, equal access, and the sovereignty of private property.

The very concept of wilderness is unfair because it is exclusionary and elitist. But to democratize wilderness is to eliminate it. The roads, bridges, causeways, parking lots, restrooms, bath houses, nature centers, and interpretive trails that ensure equal access to all are the very elements that destroy wilderness. By making wilderness accessible—by democratizing it—we transform it into a caricature of itself. It no longer is the real thing but becomes instead a model, a lifesize diorama, complete with video programs and interpretive booklets to explain to us what we see.

The true benefits of wilderness must be earned. Access must be undemocratically difficult, and any intimacy with the place must come from your own experience, initiative, and resourcefulness, not from interpretive guidebooks.

The Virginia barrier islands are among the last that offer these challenges. To reach the islands, you must go by private boat, negotiating a maze of salt marsh channels and shallow bays. There are no facilities on the islands, so you must bring whatever you need to eat or drink. There are no lifeguards to protect you from dangerous riptides, no shelter from biting insects, no one to help push your boat off a sandbar should you beach it in the wrong spot, at the wrong tide. And should you become curious about the plants of the marsh and dunes, the birds of the bays and creeks, the reptiles and fish, the insects, the history and geology of the place, you must figure things out for yourself. There are no booklets, labels, videos, or tour leaders.

But experiencing the islands as wilderness is something more than a moderate physical and intellectual challenge that eliminates the casual visitors. To appreciate the islands as wilderness, one must see the challenge as part of the reward and must want the experience deeply enough to make some sacrifices. To some, a day alone paddling a canoe through a remote marsh or hiking a desolate beach would be boring, perhaps even intimidating. For those who think otherwise, the experience can be restorative and strengthening. Not all of us want to have this experience, but for those of us who do, it is fortunate this one place remains.

While this book deals with the plants and animals of the barrier islands and salt marshes, it also is a book about people, specifically myself and my family. We have lived here for generations, since the late 1600s, and we have been sustained by this fragile system of fertile land, salt marshes, shallow bays, and remote barrier island beaches. My great-grandfather, John Badger, retired from the sea to work a seaside farm, a small parcel by today's standards of agribusiness, but with his forty cleared acres he supported a family of ten, with enough surplus profits to send his daughters to college and to help his sons buy farms of their own.

We say, in our arrogance, that we have owned land, when in fact it might be more likely that the land has owned us—at least in the stewardship aspect of ownership. Certainly the land has nurtured and supported us, and although we consider ourselves stewards of the land, the land has done more for us than we have done for it.

The best I can say is that we have done nothing to abuse the land. Over the generations, accounting for various small farms, we have left it no worse than we found it, not necessarily as a result of something we might call environmental conscience, but more as a matter of common sense. My great-grandfather, Captain John, realized that if you intended to eat the oysters growing in your marsh, then you had best not dump your chamber pot there.

Over the generations, the salt marsh landscape has woven itself through the lives of my family. I find it impossible to write about the islands and marshes without writing also about the mark they have made on our lives. Having grown up on the coast, introduced to the ocean and salt marshes at an early age by my father, I do not find it possible to stand back and regard this natural system with objectivity and detachment. After all, how could generations of people spend their lives fishing the bays, collecting clams on tidal flats, hunting the marshes, and farming the land without having the land become a part of who they are and what they believe? In a sense, land becomes family; we have depended upon it to feed us, and in turn we have tried to treat it as if it were one of us.

And there is more to it than that. While my grandparents, great-grandparents, and those who came before them made their living from the land, they lived here because they chose to, not because they had to or were expected to. Many had their youthful adventures then settled back to a pastoral life on the seaside. Old Captain John took off for the California goldfields when he was sixteen, bought a cargo-carrying schooner, and fulfilled his dream of sailing the seas. After losing his ship to the Yankees during the Civil War, he returned to the farm.

So working the land has never been a job, but a privilege, a right freely chosen. I imagine that when Captain John was a child, introduced to the islands and ocean for the first time, he felt much the same as I did when I first waded into the cold breakers, feeling their wildness and power, experiencing for the first time the open horizon, curving away to who-knows-what.

This book, then, is not just an amateur naturalist's interpretation of a barrier island and salt marsh ecosystem. For better or worse, it has a lot of me in it, not because of ego, but because I can't separate my life from that of the land and sea that surround me. Hunting rail birds in the salt marsh means more to me than a way of putting dinner on the table. I hope in reading this book you will understand why.

Clam Sign

A mud flat, left high and dry by the falling tide, is at first glance a barren place that belongs neither to the sea nor the land, a place where the grasses of the marsh will not grow, where exposed aquatic plants lie shriveling under the warm breath of spring. But these flats, so unspectacular and uninviting when seen from a distance, are teeming with life, a veritable city of strange creatures, most of which go about their business unseen and unheard just below the glistening surface of the exposed flat.

There are thousands of acres of tidal flats on the coast of Virginia where I live, and one of our spring rituals is to go clamming on the flats during the first warm days of March and April, when the rising water temperature tickles some migratory trigger in the summer flounder, and they wander in from winter haunts offshore to feed on minnows, crabs, and grass shrimp that forage in spring in the shallow bays that surround these flats. I, too, can feel the snap of the trigger, something tugging me away from the winter hearth, renewing again the seasonal need to be out there.

Clamming is a good exercise in observing life on a mud flat, because it encourages you to slow down, bend over, and pay attention. David Lewis, my frequent clamming partner, is teaching me to sign clams, which is a more sophisticated method of clamming than my usual method of pulling a rake blindly across the flat, hoping to hear the tines scrape across the hard shell of a buried clam. David is teaching me to look for clam sign, usually a small hole in the shape of a keyhole and often surrounded by tiny debris, the waste matter of a clam's digestive process.

Dave is good at signing clams, and I'm just catching on. The shellfish lie just beneath the surface of the flat, in most cases invisible except for a small hole, or actually a pair of concentric holes, through which retractable siphons draw food and expel waste. To catch a clam, you must first find these subtle signs, and then you pry out the shellfish with a clam pick, which has two metal tines approximately four inches long attached to a wooden handle.

But clam sign is not easily spotted, even for veteran signers like Dave. If the clams have not recently been feeding and expelling waste—making sign—then they are impossible to find. And even if the clams have been feeding, strong winds and currents can dismantle the little waste midden and cover the siphon hole. To complicate matters, all sorts of creatures live in the flats, and many of them make holes in the mud that look like clam sign. The upper layer of the flat is laced with tunnels and chambers laid by burrowing worms, many of which, like clams, feed by siphoning seawater through intake systems and then expelling the waste in the form of little pellets or strings.

The clam scat looks like tiny, fragile pieces of string made of mud and sand grains. They are one-eighth to one-quarter of an

inch long and are usually scattered around the siphon hole. If you can find this telltale trail of litter, you can usually find a clam.

You bend over, get on your knees, and look closely at the wet surface of the flat, which a few minutes ago had been underwater. On a good day there is plenty of sign, and you sink your pick into the mud, scrape the tines across the hard shell with a chalk-on-blackboard sound, then plant the tines under the clam and pry it loose. On bad days, when there is no sign, you rake, pulling a heavy, long-in-the-tooth garden rake across the flat, hoping for the metallic squeak of clam contact.

Pete Rew, who was our neighbor when I was growing up, said he preferred clamming to fishing any day. At the time, I was just acquainting myself with the delicious challenge of sea trout on light test line, of casting lures to chopper bluefish in the surf. Pete was in his seventies. What did he know?

I'm getting the point now, Pete. I rake the sandy bottom, and the tines scrape a heavy shell. I wedge the tines beneath the shell and pry, and with the suck of a vacuum the clam pops free, a huge, black, glossy creature the diameter of a softball, glistening in the seawater like a chunk of polished coal. These are hard clams, *Mercenaria mercenaria*, so named because the American Indians once fashioned wampum from the violet and white interior of the shell. The outer shell is grooved with growth lines like a tree trunk; it is deeply cupped, holding a fistful of golden, salty meat. A dozen of these will make a fine chowder tonight, or I'll brown some garlic in olive oil, chop the clams coarsely, and cook them with their salty juice and have them over linguini.

I'm middle-aged now, Pete. And I like clamming.

I like the grating, scraping contact of metal on shell, the pride of discovery, the illusion, perhaps, that I am somehow closer to nature by earning my dinner in this manner. I hunt. I gather.

But I enjoy, most of all, the very fact that I am here, wading on a mud flat with my trousers rolled, enjoying the cold of spring tides, the healthy suck of mud. I enjoy finding by accident the burrowing worms, the huge, predatory, knobbed whelks whose clams I am appropriating, the oystercatchers probing a nearby point of marsh, the dowitchers bobbing for worms, the raft of brant fifty yards off our flat, barking to each other like puppies.

I wonder, Pete, if these are the things you loved about clamming?

I find milky ribbon worms, which can grow to lengths of four feet, burrowing into the soft surface layer of mud. Tube worms, trumpet worms, bamboo worms, and thread worms tunnel beneath the surface I walk upon, waiting for the tide to cover their burrows so this alien will depart and they can resume feeding. Sponges, rich green sea lettuce, and branched red weeds are scattered across the flat, at the mercy of the sun and the drying breeze. When the tide ebbs, exposing the flat, the cells of the plants slam shut, sealing in precious seawater. In an hour or so the tide will again rise, the bay will cover the flat, the cells will reopen, and the plants will regain their composure and their grace, slow dancing to the silent music of the current.

In the shallow water just off the flat, flounder catch killifish, silversides, and mantis shrimp, which have been feeding on the detritus produced by the decaying marsh grass and plankton. In a few days we will drag our little minnow seine along a shallow tidal gut, catching killies, shrimp, and silversides, and then we will take the boat out to the flats, attempting to seduce a flounder with these offerings.

But now we search for our wide-bodied chowder clams, two men bent at the waist, scouring the ground for a few grains of waste left in a particular pattern by an unsuspecting bivalve.

What an amazingly efficient animal this clam is, a packet of hormones and reflexes wrapped in a calcium shell, hidden away under sand and water, its only contact with the outside world a pair of attached siphons through which the animal eats, defecates, and has sex.

Those seem to be the clam's only functions—to eat, grow, and reproduce—and it is very good at all three. Larval clams float with the currents until they near metamorphosis, and then they anchor themselves to the bottom, extend a muscular foot, and burrow into the bottom, which will be their permanent home. From then on, the clam becomes a total recluse, functioning solely through its pair of siphons.

As they grow, many young clams undergo a sex change. At one year, clams are functional males, although their permanent sexual identity is not yet determined. In the next year or two the clams will mature and become either male or female at about a one-to-one ratio.

The clam feeds by filtering phytoplankton, bacteria, detritus, and dissolved organic material from sea water. The incurrent siphon, which brings in nutrients, has tiny tentacles along its rim that sort out possible food particles. The tentacles act as the off/on switch for the incurrent siphon. When there are plenty of nutrients suspended in the current, the tentacles tell the clam to go into the feeding mode; if the seawater is clouded with suspended particles of sand, mud, and other large debris, the tentacles shut the system down.

Seawater is pumped into the clam by the gills, and food particles attach to the gills in a thick mucus solution. Hairlike cilia on the gills move the food particles slowly toward the mouth, where palpi that line the entrance further sort out the food particles, deciding which will be ingested and which will be rejected.

Rejected particles are moved by cilia from the palpi and gills and are collected in the mantle cavity. When a sufficient quantity of waste accumulates it is ejected as pseudofeces in loose, mucousy strings.

The clam's digestive system also plays a role in reproduction. When the water temperature rises in the spring, male clams release semen through their feeding siphons. The semen, which contains pheromones, is spread over the flat by the currents and is ingested by female clams. The pheromones stimulate the females to release eggs, which they expel through their excurrent siphon. Each egg, supported by a gelatinous envelope, floats freely in the current until it is eventually attacked by spermatozoa. As the embryo develops in the first few hours of life, it becomes covered with cilia, which eventually tear apart the gelatinous capsule. The fertilized egg then floats along on the current as the larva develops.

The larvae will float freely in the seawater, forming a vital part of the detritus/zooplankton soup of the estuary. After twelve to fourteen days, the larvae that survive will begin their metamorphosis into seed clams. The shell thickens and a byssal gland develops; this gland secretes a tough thread, enabling the seed clam to anchor itself on the substrate. The tiny clam (0.3 to 0.4 millimeters long) does not burrow at this stage, but attaches itself to sand grains, small rocks, or shells with its byssal thread. The attachment is not permanent; the clam can sever its link and move on to habitat more to its liking should it prefer.

What the seed clams are looking for at this point in their young lives is water of proper salinity and a bottom that will be a good home for the adult clam. Clams grow best in seawater containing from about twenty to thirty-five parts per thousand (ppt) of salt. In fact, the larval clam will not begin its metamorphosis to seed clam unless the salinity is at least eighteen to

twenty ppt, ensuring that the seed clam will not set in an area where the salinity is unsuitable for adults.

Clams also prefer a bottom substrate of sand or mud, and this is what the larval clam or seed clam looks for. The clam's favorite habitat is a sandy bottom in a shallow estuary where the current moves the water at a fairly leisurely pace. Clams don't like the fast-moving water of inlets, nor do they like turbid waters where the bottom has been disturbed. Although they feed on suspended food particles, excessive turbidity can clog their filtering systems and eventually kill the clams.

The remarkable thing about the clam's odyssey is that it reproduces, grows, avoids predators, selects a healthy home environment, and develops a discriminatory palate without conscious thought. The clam has no brain. It is a digestive and reproductive system unhobbled by fear, conscience, greed, envy, ambition. All it knows is food and sex. Hence, perhaps, the saying "Happy as a clam."

Clams are wonderfully fecund. Give her a whiff of good old male hormone, and the female starts pumping out eggs in great billowing clouds. Get a few males and females together on a tidal flat when the water temperature is right, and you'll have a clam orgy that can turn the water smoky with eggs and sperm.

A female clam is at the peak of her sexual prowess when she is three years old and measures about sixty millimeters in length. A healthy female in the wild will release sixteen to twenty-four million eggs during the spawning season, which on the Virginia coast runs from May through August. In laboratory tests, large, chowder-sized females have produced more than fifty million eggs per season. Of course, only a small percentage of the eggs survive to become adult clams. The eggs, spermatozoa, and clam larvae all become part of the zooplankton carried by the currents through the estuary, which in summer provides a nutrient-rich soup for a wide variety of animals. Scientists say that in a shallow seaside estuary during the summer months, there can be as many as thirty million clam larvae per square meter.

Most of the larvae are eaten by fish, crabs, birds, and other mollusks. Even clams eat their own eggs and larvae by filtering them out of seawater. The clam's vulnerability decreases as it outgrows the army of predators. Once the clam becomes an adult and burrows into the bottom, the predators become fairly specific. Mud crabs, blue crabs, and green crabs dig clams out of the sediment, crushing the smaller shells with their claws and chipping off the edges of larger shells.

Several mollusks feed on adult clams. Oyster drills and moon snails drill holes in the shells and remove the clam's tissues. A whelk will chip off the edges of the clam's shell, then insert its proboscises through the opening and eat the living tissue. The sea star pulls the shells of the clam apart and inserts its stomach into the cavity, digesting the contents.

So the remarkable fecundity of the clam is not wasted. The billions of eggs and larvae are vital to the salt marsh food chain, and the adult clams that survive provide food for a variety of birds, fish, shellfish, and mollusks. Indeed, the clam nurtures the entire range of salt marsh life, beginning with microscopic animals and ending with those of us who search the tidal flats for clam sign, hoping to find some subtle evidence of life, some manifestation of things not readily seen.

Spartina

I've always liked to go hiking on marshes, especially the upper marsh where the tides reach only during storms, where wetland gradually gives way to upland. This narrow buffer that separates highland from marsh is a great place to go exploring, especially after the high tides of a northeaster. The tides wash up all manner of treasures. I've found old decoys, colorful crab pot floats, broken oars, and weathered driftwood in abstract patterns that make me want to try woodcarving.

But the best thing about hiking a marsh is that I always have it to myself. When people go for afternoon hikes, even here on the coast, they seldom go on the marsh. We've been taught in our culture to avoid marshes and swamps. There is something sinister about a marsh, something forbidding. People distrust places where the footing is not always solid and reliable. We like dependability and certainty; we like knowing what to expect when we put our feet down.

Marshes have been unfairly maligned in our society for centuries. I think of bad guys in old Tarzan movies who sink forever into swampy mud pits. There's the image of Humphrey Bogart covered with leeches in *The African Queen. Swamp Thing. The Creature from the Swamp.* . . . Nothing good comes from a marsh, only evil and death. Marshes are filled with poisonous snakes, disease-carrying insects, foul smells, and labyrinthine waterways where one can become lost forever.

Such attitudes, still widely held and perpetuated in our culture, helped bring about the destruction of hundreds of thousands of acres of marshlands in America in the last century. Marshland was wasteland, and to conquer it—to reclaim it as farmland, homesite, garbage dump, industrial park—was a noble undertaking. In fine American tradition, we took something we believed to be of no worth, and through hard work and perseverance, we made it useful and productive.

Although in our minds we now know better, in our hearts we still distrust marshes. Given the choice between a marsh and something of more evident value—a motel or marina, perhaps—most local governments and planning commissions, reflecting the will of their constituents, would opt for the latter. Motels and marinas we know, marshes are still too mysterious, their value still too blurred. The Swamp Creature is with us still.

As the legal debate over protecting tidal marshes raged in the 1970s, scientists produced numerous studies demonstrating the remarkable fecundity and usefulness of a marsh. We now know that the biomass produced annually by a natural marsh rivals that of America's most fertile and chemically manipulated farmland. Marshes are responsible for millions of dollars worth of fish and shellfish, which support coastal economies and help feed the world. Marshes protect the mainland from storms. Marshes filter contaminants from surface water and return it to aquifers in a more pure state.

To provide legal protection to salt marshes, it was necessary to prove that they offer substantial tangible benefits to humans, that they do their part in our free-market economy, providing food, jobs, clean water, recreation, and flood protection. Few arguments were made that marshes should be protected because of their inherent beauty or their biological diversity, or because they represent the last of the coastal wilderness, the only remaining east coast ecoscape unmarked by pavement.

The wilderness value of a vast salt marsh is no less, it seems to me, than the mountain ranges of the West, which normally come to mind when someone speaks of wilderness. The same arguments for preserving mountain ranges as wilderness can also be applied to salt marshes. Indeed, a salt marsh wilderness is more fragile and vulnerable, its subtle beauty more easily marred, than that of mountains.

The highest value of a natural salt marsh lies in its wildness, its ability to offer momentary escape from the world humans have created, a place where nature is in control. I enjoy hiking a marsh or canoeing its creeks because it provides the same surprises, the same sense of discovery, as any other wilderness setting.

The vegetated marsh is surprisingly firm, its dark soil knitted by the complex roots of cordgrass, *Spartina alterniflora*, the dominant plant species of coastal marshes throughout the United States. The soil is also matted with the decaying leaves and stems of *Spartina*, especially in the higher marshes, where the tides reach only now and then to sweep away plant litter. Underfoot there are ribbed mussels, growing in clusters amid the roots of *Spartina*. And there is *Salicornia*, or saltwort, a tubular, succulent little plant that the old-timers used to pickle in vinegar to use as a relish. Dark gray fiddler crabs, the males waving one huge claw in a phallic advertisement, scurry through the grass and disappear into burrows. Marsh periwinkles crawl up the stalks of *Spartina*, scraping nutrients from the surface of the grass. And you find surprises: a broken shell of a willet egg, tan and spotted with brown and purple; the carapace of a horseshoe crab; a midden of shells left by oystercatchers in a favorite feeding spot; the nest of a clapper rail in the high grass on the edge of a creek; shiny black egg casings of skates, called mermaid's purses; and chains of egg casings of channeled whelks, which look from a distance like discarded snakeskins.

What you don't find in the marsh are mutant swamp creatures, evil-smelling gases, venomous reptiles, and plague-carrying insects. A healthy marsh smells good, the odor of a giant food factory at work: photosynthesis, cell division, cell decay, the attack of bacteria on cellulose, egg production, egg consumption, millions of larvae, countless millions of new lives, deaths, transformations, the sharing of energy, the passing of life from plant to animal, from animal to plant, the sustenance and substance of life.

On the Virginia marshes, there are few, if any, venomous reptiles. Cottonmouth moccasins range only as far northward as the extreme southeastern corner of the state. We have several species of harmless water snakes, which often are taken for moccasins and are treated accordingly. There are more disease-carrying insects in most suburban backyards than in the salt marshes. A few mosquitoes on a calm day, a few green-headed flies, but a walk in the woods will expose you to many more biting bugs than will a walk in the marsh.

The marshes do have their mysteries. How, for example, is a grass such as *Spartina* able to survive in an environment that would bring quick death to nearly any other plant? *Spartina* seems to thrive on the salt water of the estuary, growing tallest and thickest along the edges of creeks, where its roots are immersed twice daily, its stems washed by the flowing tides. It is a remarkable plant, irrigated by pure seawater, engineered to withstand violent coastal storms, a processor and distributor of solar energy upon which the entire estuary depends.

On the salt marsh, *Spartina alterniflora* is ubiquitous. Along the edges of creeks and bays, it grows in thick stands sometimes to heights of six feet. On the upper marsh, where tidal flow is limited, the grass is shorter, from about six inches to two or three feet, and it grows less dense, often with colonies of *Salicornia*. In the upper elevations, where the salt marsh joins fastland, *Spartina alterniflora* gives way to *Spartina patens*, a shorter, thicker grass called saltmeadow hay, and *Distichlis spicata*, or salt grass.

The entire community of marshes, bays, islands, fish, shellfish, birds, and animals begins here with these grasses that form the basis of the salt marsh food chain, collecting the energy of the sun in photosynthesis and later distributing it to myriad creatures as the grasses die and are broken down by bacteria. The mixture of bacteria, epiphytic algae, and the cellulose particles of digested *Spartina* forms the broad base of the salt marsh food chain, a nutrient-rich soup called detritus.

It is a remarkable but very economical process perfected over centuries of natural selection. Nothing is superfluous. Nothing is left to waste. The system is fragile but perfectly balanced. The plants grow prodigiously during the summer, fed by nutrients swept in with the tides, storing the energy of the sun through photosynthesis during the long, unshaded days. Then in the fall this stored energy is released as the exposed stems and leaves die. The plant collapses to the marsh floor, and the bacteria

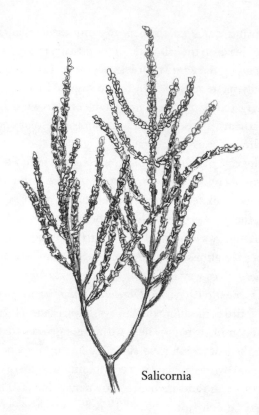

Salicornia

attack. The single-cell bacteria are so small that they cannot consume bits of *Spartina* in the traditional manner. Instead, the plant is digested outside the cells of the animals, and as a result, the *Spartina* is reduced to progressively smaller bits and pieces.

This rich detritus mixture—bacteria, plant remains, larvae, free-flowing eggs, and algae, all stirred by tidal action into a nutritious broth—is eaten by protozoans that live in the shallow water; by the filter-feeding, burrowing worms of the tidal flats; and by oysters, clams, mussels, nematodes, snails, insect larvae, fiddler crabs, and small fish such as menhaden and mullet, which either filter the nutrients from the water or eat them with bottom mud.

Clams burrow beneath the bottom and send up a pair of siphons, one of which pulls detritus-rich seawater through its digestive system while the other expels small, nondigestible particles and waste. Most of the filter feeders consume detritus in this manner, sucking the broth through hairlike cilia, membranes, or, in the case of the marsh mussel, a mesh of mucous threads covering the gills.

Fiddler crabs eat detritus by picking up gobs of it with their claws, then sorting out the digestible particles with six specially adapted legs that cover their mouths. The tiny legs are shaped like paddles and are covered with stiff bristles, which sort the large particles of food from the small. The small particles are digested, but the larger pieces are temporarily stored in a predigestive chamber and, when they accumulate, are spit back into a claw and returned to the surface of the marsh.

If you hike a high marsh or walk along an exposed tidal flat, you will see several species of snails. Mud snails forage along the surface of the flat, scraping detritus from the surface with their radulae, rasplike teeth that pull food particles into their mouths. The marsh periwinkle feeds on the lower stems of *Spartina*, scraping away algae and detritus that have collected on the plants.

The detritus eaters are preyed upon by animals higher on the food chain: larger fish, blue crabs, waterfowl, wading birds, raccoons, and other mammals. A clapper rail stalks the cordgrass marsh, spearing an unsuspecting periwinkle snail from a grass stem. A great blue heron waits patiently in a shallow gut, then surprises a passing killifish. An osprey circles over the open creek,

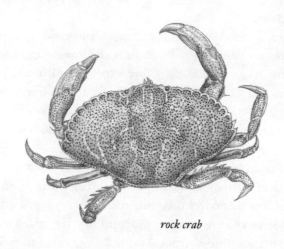

rock crab

green crab

fiddler crab

ghost crab

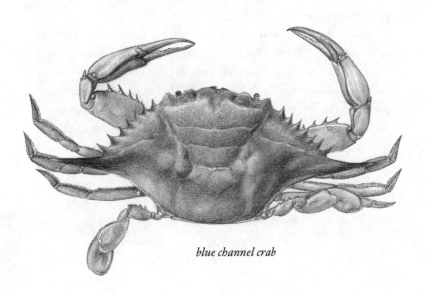

blue channel crab

dives, and comes up with a mullet in its talons. A fisherman drifts in a small boat along a tidal creek, hoping to entice a flounder with an offering of squid and minnows.

While the salt marsh food chain begins with the sun and the *Spartina* grasses, the remarkable thing about the marsh is that these plants are able to function at all, much less begin a process that gives life to creatures ranging from one-celled animals to humans. The salt water would literally suck the life out of less-adapted plants, were they to find their way to the marsh. Through the process of osmosis, nature attempts to balance the concentration of particles suspended in water by moving a less-concentrated solution through a membrane to a more-concentrated one. If a freshwater plant suddenly found itself in salt water, the water contained in the plant's cells would be drawn through the plant's membranes toward the more concentrated salt water until the concentrations became equal. In a very brief time, the fresh water contained in the plant would be removed, and the plant would die.

Spartina has solved this problem by allowing a certain amount of salt to enter its cells, bringing the salt content of the water within the plant to a slightly higher concentration than that of the surrounding seawater. In this manner, the osmotic pressure is reversed; instead of fresh water moving away from the plant cells, seawater attempts to enter, inflating the plant cells and giving them strength and resiliency.

Spartina, however, is selective with regard to the salts it allows to enter, and it screens out those that might harm the plant. The most common sea salt, sodium chloride, is allowed to pass, as is a small amount of potassium, which is an important nutrient for the grass. The salts are screened by a cellulose covering the plant's roots. Excess and unneeded salts are concentrated on the membrane and are washed away by seawater and rain as it leaches into the soil. Other excess salts are secreted onto the leaves of the plant through special glands on the upper surfaces of the leaves. On a dry summer day, a tiny coating of salt crystals will make the *Spartina* leaves shimmer in the sunlight. The crystals did not dry on the leaves as seawater evaporated but instead came from within the plant as it attempted to maintain its perfect pitch of osmotic pressure.

Spartina, like most land plants, draws moisture from the soil as water evaporates from its leaves. The plant breathes in carbon dioxide through stomata, cells in its leaves that open during the day when the plant is active, then close at night to conserve water. Water evaporates while the stomata are open during the day, and as it does, water is pulled from the soil to replace it, much as someone might suck a soft drink through a straw. The water is transported through xylem, thin columns filled with spongy tissues, and the evaporative pressure placed on the water column helps give the plant strength.

Living in a saltwater environment is not the only challenge *Spartina* must overcome. The plant lives in a dense soil very low in oxygen, which it needs to survive, and it must compete for this scarce element with millions of bacteria and higher organisms that live in the upper layers of the soil. *Spartina* has solved its oxygen problem with intercalary canals, a series of air passages that transmits oxygen brought in through the stomata in the leaves down to the roots, where it is needed. If you pull a *Spartina alterniflora* plant, you will usually see reddish mud adjacent to some of the roots. This is caused by oxygen reacting with iron sulfide in the soil to produce iron oxide, or rust.

So *Spartina* survives in a hostile environment by using to its advantage the salt that would kill other plants, creating a positive osmotic pressure that inflates the plant and strengthens it. And while water is carried upward from the roots through the xylem, oxygen molecules are moved downward through intercalary canals. But while several chemical and physical mechanisms allow *Spartina* to thrive in salt water and to feed oxygen to its roots, it still must overcome another problem presented by the estuary: the daily buffeting of the tides, as well as occasional violent storms.

Spartina lives in a physically demanding environment. The marsh has no windbreaks, so the breezes bend the slender stems at will. During storms the ocean can breach the barrier islands and break directly upon the marsh, sending tons of water crashing upon the shafts of *Spartina*. Even on normal days, the twice-daily high tides flood the marsh, bending the grasses in a fast-moving current.

So *Spartina* must first of all be solidly anchored, which it achieves by sending tough rhizomes through the muddy soil and interlocking root systems with other plants, finding strength not as individuals but as colonies of plants that survive or perish together.

And the shafts of the plants must be resilient and tough, willing to bend but reluctant to break. *Spartina* accomplishes this with the same mechanisms it uses to survive in salt water. By adjusting its osmotic pressure so that its cells are always fully inflated, the plant functions like a tire inner tube, able to withstand great shock before puncturing. And the thin column of water contained in the xylem, drawn constantly through the roots by evaporation taking place on the leaves, helps make the plant flexible but extremely strong.

The stems of *Spartina* are also engineered for strength. Cut one off and you'll see a tube within a tube, precisely separated by cellulose spacers. The stems carry no water or gases; their only function is one of support, and they run all the way from the seed head downward to the underground rhizomes.

Spartina is a wonder of chemistry, physics, and structural engineering. While most plants would wilt within hours of being placed in its environment, *Spartina* thrives, and because of its remarkable adaptability, it has its particular part of the marsh nearly all to itself. *Salicornia*, the only other plant common in the lower marsh, seems to complement *Spartina* rather than compete with it. *Salicornia* is a tiny plant, and it seems at home growing among the thin stands of *Spartina* away from the water's edge.

Spartina defines the topography of the lower tidal marsh, where salt water inundates the plants twice daily. It is a precarious landscape, where only a few inches in elevation separate *Spartina alterniflora* from its smaller, finer cousin, *Spartina patens*, a plant of the higher marsh where tides reach only during the highest periods of the monthly cycles. Each plant has its niche, well defined and precise: *Spartina alterniflora* on the lowest marshes, followed by *Spartina patens;* the three species of *Salicornia* we have on the Virginia coast; *Distichlis spicata*, or salt grass, similar in appearance to *Spartina patens;* sea lavender, with its tiny, blue summer flowers; sea oxeye, a striking succulent plant with yellow flowers in summer and brown, prickly seed heads in winter; marsh elder; groundsel; and, on the lowest fastland, bay myrtle and cedar.

This range of salt marsh plant species may occur over a change in elevation of one foot or less, and subtle changes in sea level bring about dramatic differences in plant communities. In recent years, sea level has been rising, and on a low-lying seaside farm where my father grew up, a sweet potato field he tended as a boy is now upper marsh, with a nice stand of *Spartina patens*. Some day it will likely be a *Spartina alterniflora* marsh.

Salt marshes were for many years considered the enemy, one of those elements of nature that needed to be conquered, and even now we still do not know much about them. We know that marshes help to purify water, but what role do the grasses such as *Spartina* play, for example, in processing heavy metals and other pollutants?

Will the salt marshes one day feed us? A five-year project in the coastal desert of Mexico has shown that a salt marsh plant, *Salicornia bigelovii*, can be cultivated, irrigated with seawater, and its seeds processed to make a high protein meal and low saturated fat oil for use in poultry feed. As the world population grows and its fresh water supply becomes increasingly scarce, the idea of an oilseed crop irrigated with salt water has exciting potential.

We tend to evaluate the salt marsh with an anthropocentric currency. If it has high value for humans, then let's protect it. And the more we learn about the salt marshes, the more varied their benefits become, the greater their potential, the closer the relationship between the health and welfare of humans and that of the ecosystem. The fact that one of the benefits is the very intangible value of coastal wilderness may even one day take hold.

Flounder Season

Ernest Hemingway wrote in *Big Two-Hearted River* of fishing as a form of catharsis, of healing. And so it is with flounder, a fish that here on the coast symbolizes the promise of a new season and new life. The first flounder of the year signals not only the beginning of the fishing season, but a general rebirth of the salt marsh, even among those of us who drift our boats across the shallow bays, trailing baits of minnow and squid, traditional offerings for these migrants who in late March move in from the open ocean to forage in the warming waters of the shallow flats.

The flounder is an unlikely hero, a peculiar choice as a symbol of rebirth and renewed hope. It is neither sleek nor handsome, but a predator that relies on deceit rather than superior strength, speed, or cunning. The flounder is a bottom dweller whose brown, splotchy top side is designed to blend in with the dark, muddy bottom of the estuary. Both eyes are on the same side of the head, giving the fish the appearance that its development might have been arrested during some painful and awkward point of evolution.

Give or take a few million years, the flounder could be either fish or amphibian. It could puff up to a full three-dimensional figure, sprout legs, and take off through the marsh, zapping flies with a sticky frog tongue.

The flounder is a victory of substance over style, proof that in nature beauty is relative, and usually accidental. The flounder's function is to lie in wait on a muddy bay bottom, and its form helps it fill that function perfectly. Drift across a shallow flat when the water is clear and try to spy a flounder on the bottom. As long as the fish remains still, it is almost invisible.

The flounder's great value is that it gives us our first excuse of the year to leave the warmth of home and hearth and get out there, to be buffeted by spring northeasters, to endure the wet and cold and fishless days sane people avoid. The first flounder of spring is cause for celebration, because it is a tangible reminder that the cycle of seasons grinds on, ensuring us that the gray days of winter are retreating and that better times lie ahead.

So we bundle up in sweaters and windbreakers and head out, comforted by hot coffee. After spending the winter off the coast, the flounder move to the estuaries in early spring, searching for food in the shallow bays, where the sun begins to warm the water, bringing to life the killifish, grass shrimp, and small crabs. We spend the early part of the season here, in small bays such as Burton's Bay and Cedar Island Bay, which are typical of the estuaries that separate the barrier islands from the mainland. The bays are very shallow, with soft, muddy bottoms punctuated by oyster rocks laid bare by the falling tide. Most of the oysters are planted by watermen, who will harvest them when they reach market size. Oysters are sessile animals, meaning they tend to cluster in permanent communities, unmoving until they are pried loose and taken to market. Discarded shells help build the oyster rocks. The shallow mounds of shell provide a firm, protective footing for young oysters, or spat. Plant a few mounds of empty shells, and the following season you'll see live, young oysters attached to them, beginning a shellfish community that will in a few more seasons be very valuable.

The flats where the oysters live are fertile places that become flush with life as the spring sun warms the water, awakening the tens of thousands of marine animals that spent the winter buried in the soft blanket of the muddy bottom.

The flounder, of course, are aware of this, and they come in through the inlets, navigate the deep tidal creeks, and finally find their way to the shallow bays and begin their banquet. We follow the flounder. We drift along the bays in a small skiff, letting the wind and tide push us as we trail our baits of minnow and squid. Sometimes the flounder strikes violently, but more often it is subtle, picking up the bait as a shopper might inspect a head of lettuce in the food market. These little examinations are difficult to detect, especially when your bait is bouncing along the bottom. Sometimes it registers as a gentle pull, an unexpected heaviness, and at other times it is the opposite, a sudden lifting as the fish swims toward you with the bait.

You set the hook, lifting sharply with the rod, and if the fish is there the line will go tight, peeling from the reel in spasmodic jabs and jerks. The flounder does not run like a bluefish or weakfish but retreats to the bottom, slugging it out in short, powerful bursts, using its thick body to best advantage.

The flounder is slow to retreat or capitulate. Once we had a six-pounder that had been on ice for thirty minutes give a great heave, slam open the lid of the fish box, and somersault over the gunwale of the boat to its freedom.

While the flounder is rather homely looking, its flesh is as white as new snow and its flavor is just as delicate. My father insisted that flounder should be skinned before cooking, and the act of cleaning fish was to him a ritual of surgical precision. He would use a short, stiff blade to make a skin-deep incision around the perimeter of the fish's body, then with a pair of pliers he would lift a corner of skin, get a good grip, and pull the skin away, leaving a wonderful slab of fish meat. The trick in skinning a flounder, he told me, is to make a precise incision along the edges of the fish. The incision should penetrate the skin but not go into the flesh; otherwise the flesh will pull away with the skin.

After skinning the fish, my father would use the stiff knife to cut along each side of the dorsal and anal fins; then he would grip the fins with the pliers and pull them away in a ribbon. He would remove the head and tail and flush the body cavity with water, and the flounder would be ready to cook. He liked to grill it over charcoal, basting it with melted butter and lemon juice.

The flounder will spend a month or two, depending upon water temperature, in the shallow bays, and then they will retreat to the deeper waters of the creeks and inlets that separate the barrier islands. Fishing in the bays can be difficult, because they are shallow and littered with oyster rocks that can do serious damage to the propeller of an outboard. We seldom go fishing without running aground a few times. Spend enough time flounder fishing, and you get a good lesson in the dynamics of the estuary.

Cedar Island and Burton's bays are separated by a narrow body of water called Teagle's Ditch, which is not really a ditch at all, but an opening between two huge salt marshes, a narrow channel dug long ago to join these two seaside bays. On the north side of the opening is Cedar Island Bay, and on the south is Burton's Bay.

Because the currents are very strong in Teagle's Ditch, the water is deep, the bottom scoured of silt and soft sediment by the scrubbing of the tides. The bays, however, are a different story. They are wide and shallow, and the tidal currents move in a very gradual ebb and flow. When water moves slowly, the bits and pieces of plant matter, sand, topsoil, and other debris suspended in water settle slowly to the bottom. It is not until the moving water is constricted in a narrow passage such as Teagle's Ditch that it picks up enough velocity to keep all those suspended particles moving along.

So on the seaside, the wide bays that separate the barrier islands from the mainland are very shallow and the water moves slowly. The narrow creeks are deep, sculpted by moving water.

A channel crosses the seaside bays, but it is neither deep nor permanent. Its approximate position is shown by the red and green markers erected years ago by the Coast Guard. In Burton's Bay the channel is perhaps four feet deep, and the surrounding water is less than one foot at low tide. As an old waterman once told me, "Son, there's a lot of water out there, but it's stretched mighty thin."

The channel running through Burton's Bay and Cedar Island Bay is not a natural part of the seaside topography; it was dug during the 1960s by the U.S. Army Corps of Engineers as part of the Intracoastal Waterway system of the Atlantic coast. The Intracoastal Waterway was designed to allow boaters to travel along the coast without having to enter the ocean. Taking advantage of the protection afforded by the barrier islands that line the coast from Long Island south, the waterway snakes through the marshes and bays that separate the islands from the mainland. Planners designed the waterway around existing creeks, rivers, and bays, then tied them together with manmade channels. The result is a meandering estuarine trail that follows deep tidal creeks, cuts across shallow bays, and sometimes follows a straight, machine-cut channel through a high marsh.

The purpose of the Intracoastal Waterway was to create a safe, sheltered passage for small recreational and commercial boats. Boaters could embark in New York, for example, and sail all the way to Miami, and the only open water they would face would be at the mouths of several bays, such as the Delaware and the Chesapeake.

The portion of the waterway that runs behind the Virginia barrier islands is called the Virginia Inside Passage. Teagle's Ditch and the wandering channel through Burton's and Cedar Island bays are part of it, although the government seems to have lost interest in performing the necessary maintenance dredging to keep it open. When the waterway was completed in the early 1960s, the Corps and the local waterway committee probably reasoned that the Inside Passage would be a low-maintenance project. Cut a swath through a marsh, connect two large bays, and you have a quick and convenient passageway. Repeat the process enough times, and you have a passageway along the entire coast. The channel will be deeper than the surrounding bay, a greater volume of water will move through it, and it will maintain its depth, much as Teagle's Ditch does.

But shortly after the project was completed, the new channels through the shallow bays began to fill with silt, and rather than being a one-time, low-maintenance project, the Corps found that waterway maintenance was frequent and costly. Many areas had to be dredged every few years or the channels would fill in completely, making passage impossible for all but the smallest shallow-draft boats. And in the thirty years since the Virginia

Inside Passage was built, we've become much more aware of the importance of marshes and tidal flats to the estuarine ecosystem and hence to the local economy. So even if the government were willing to spend the money for frequent maintenance dredging, there is the question of what to do with the dredge spoil. Dumping it on a nearby salt marsh, the most common disposal method of the 1960s, is no longer permitted, and disposal underwater can foul valuable clam and oyster beds. As a result, in recent years dredging has been kept to the minimum necessary for local navigation. Large boats sailing the Intracoastal Waterway now travel the Chesapeake Bay, using the C&D Canal in Delaware, which links the Chesapeake with the Delaware River and Delaware Bay.

No one is sure why the seaside bays have filled so dramatically in the past half century. There likely are a number of causes: alteration of the natural movement of water through the estuary; an increase in mechanized farming on the mainland, encouraging the runoff of topsoil and nutrients through the watersheds; the ditching of marshes and the damming of watersheds, slowing the velocity and decreasing the carrying capacity of water; an increase in boat traffic and the introduction during this century of the motorboat, whose prop wash scours mud and other debris from the soft edges of creeks; and the disappearance in the 1930s of the vast eelgrass beds, which had helped stabilize the bottom and trap sediment.

The watershed system of the seaside is like a complex system of veins and arteries. Tiny ditches and streams drain rainwater from towns, residential neighborhoods, and farms many miles from the bays and marshes. These ditches and streams flow into larger ditches and streams and finally into a seaside creek, where the freshwater runoff is mixed with the tidal water of the estuary. The creek flows into bays, through marshes, and finally into an inlet between the barrier islands and thus into the Atlantic.

The watershed flow and the tidal currents are like slow-moving passenger trains, and the ticket holders include bits of sand, silt, plankton, decaying organic matter, clay particles from cut-over woodland, and topsoils and nutrients from farm fields. Fresh water can carry a heavier load than salt water can, so when the suspended debris is flushed into the seaside bays, it settles to the bottom as the water's salinity increases and its velocity decreases.

When I run aground while drifting across a tidal flat for flounder, I am reminded that the estuary is a dynamic organism and that it is a product of its constituent parts. The health of the bay cannot be separated from the health of the creek, the watershed stream, the salt marsh, the islands, the ocean. These are all interconnected and interdependent.

I am reminded, too, that I am part of the system, a fisherman who clumsily attempts to find my supper in the estuary. The estuary feeds me, and my health depends upon its vitality and prolificacy.

Perhaps that is the real reason we come out here on these cold March and April days: to renew the bond between our lives and that of the marsh. It is not simply the pull of the fish we are after. We are looking for proof and reassurance that we really do belong here, that this is the framework that supports our fragile lives.

Life at the Edge

I have nothing against mountains, but I prefer sand to rocks, subtlety to stridency. Mountains are too imposing, too overstated, like geology flexing its muscles. I prefer instead the fragments of mountains—quartz, garnet, magnetite—washed down from the highlands to the coast, mixed with the calcium fragments of seashells and deposited in a narrow ribbon at the edge of the sea.

That is the stuff these islands are made of: the remains of ancient mountains, the remains of shells, geological wreckage that takes on a new life in this mysterious edge where land meets sea. The sand of these islands seems organic, with a life of its own, forever changing like an amoeba, constantly altering itself in response to pressures from outside.

In this particular place, given the kinetic energy of the ocean and the inertia of land, change is a matter of survival. The islands change daily, by the minute, by the second. Sand is slowly carried from the continental shelf toward the mainland and is deposited as offshore bars. Waves carry sand as they break upon the beach, and because waves usually strike the land at an angle, a longshore current is created. This current moves sand parallel to the beach in what is called *littoral drift*. Along most of the east coast, the drift moves in a north-south direction, carrying sand from northern islands to southern ones.

While sand is constantly being moved by wave action and the longshore current, wind also has an effect, building and erasing dunes or helping to feed the longshore current by sending dry sand into the ocean with offshore breezes.

These three elements—sea, sand, and wind—work together to achieve something of a dynamic balance. The topography of barrier islands is never fixed; change is expected and is a natural part of the process, and this energy that brings about change is what protects the mainland, especially during storms, when a great deal of energy is concentrated in a small area over a relatively brief time. During northeast storms or hurricanes, new inlets can be cut between barrier islands, existing inlets can be closed, dunes can be flattened by both wind and water, and entire islands can be temporarily converted into sandbars. While the immediate effects may appear devastating, such alterations in the landscape are the islands' means of absorbing the energy of the ocean, especially when it is magnified by storm tides, heavy seas, and strong winds.

It is the nature of the islands to constantly change their profile, much to the frustration of cartographers and mariners, who prefer their channels and coastal inlets to stay put for a reasonable length of time. But the islands are alive in the sense that they respond to what is around them, which always is the sea and frequently is the product of man.

The barrier islands are like a giant rubber buffer that separates a force in motion, the sea, from an object that is at rest, the land. By acquiescing to the forces of the sea, by changing and flowing with the sea's energy as if they were water itself, the islands survive and thus protect the object at rest from the kinetic force.

Geologists call the phenomenon island migration; developers call it erosion. If someone builds a house on an island, intending it to be more or less permanent, they will find that sooner or later the island will squirm out from under it, leaving it at the mercy of the sea. The builder must then move the house to the island's new address and be prepared to repeat the process every few years.

Building on beaches is a relatively new phenomenon. The American Indians, who seemed to have a better understanding than we of the sea's edge, built their villages in the forested upland portions of the islands, well removed from daily Sturm und Drang of the three elements. Early settlers, perhaps taking a lesson from the Indians, did the same. It was not until the Civil War era that we decided that the hostility of the sea edge was no match for American technology; we wanted to live on the beach, so we would tame those elements that our grandfathers feared and respected.

The battle has raged for a century and a half. The sea edge insists on being dynamic, while we demand that it stay in one place for a reasonable length of time. Though we have fought a good fight, victory has yet eluded us.

Often, if enough houses are built on an island, it becomes easier and cheaper to put sand under the houses rather than to move the houses to where the sand happens to be. In resort cities along the coast, taxpayers spend millions of dollars to fund "beach replenishment" projects, in which huge pumps suck sand from the bottom of the Atlantic and deposit it along the developed beachfront.

And on resort beaches, more millions in taxpayers' money are used to hire bulldozers to build tall sand dunes to separate the beach from the houses, hotels, and other businesses. The dunes give property owners a great feeling of security, as if those sandy, manmade mountains are protecting them from the petulance of the sea. But they find, after a rigorous northeast storm, that the ocean can reduce their mountains to overwash fans in the space of a single high-tide cycle. And that, of course, is what the islands intended all along; any manmade mountain of sand near the surf zone is by definition temporary.

Barrier beaches have survived for all these centuries not by challenging the ocean but by accommodating it. Wild beaches and offshore bars, such as those along the Virginia coast, are low, wide, and dynamic, and when a storm hits, its energy is dissipated over a wide expanse of low beach. The ocean flows over the island, flattening temporary dunes, carrying nutrients to the leeward salt marshes, creating vast shell-laden plains where in the spring terns and plovers will nest.

Barrier beaches are unstable by design. Sand moves as readily as the water and wind, and to stop the beaches from moving is as pointless as trying to halt the ocean current or stop the wind from blowing.

In a natural barrier island and estuarine system, the only constant is an elemental balance, which is tested daily by sea level and the pulse of the tides. On the beach, every inch counts. In a storm, an area a few inches lower than its surroundings might become an overwash fan; and if the storm is persistent and violent, it might even become a new inlet. An area a few inches higher

than its surroundings might support a stand of beach grass, which will trap sand and encourage the area to grow even higher, becoming a small dune. An area a few inches higher than its surroundings will provide safe nesting areas for colonies of plovers, terns, and skimmers. Birds that build in low areas are likely to lose their eggs or chicks to high tides should there be a storm during the nesting cycle.

The changing nature of barrier beaches is easily seen. A swim in the surf provides immediate evidence. You place your beach towel and sunglasses on the berm of the beach, dive into the breakers, tread water for a few minutes, and find that you have moved several dozen yards south from where your towel and glasses lie. Your trip was courtesy of the local longshore current, which, while it transported you along the beach, was providing the same service for billions and billions of grains of sand, many of which have by now found their way into your swimsuit.

If you swim back to the beach and retrieve your towel, you'll find that it is gritty with sand, thanks to the breeze that keeps those tiny crystals of quartz and feldspar moving along. If the wind was really blowing, your towel would be completely covered with sand, and you might not even find it until the wind changed direction and began herding the grains of sand to another destination.

The islands change constantly, and these changes manifest themselves in both near-term and long-term ways. A swimmer can feel the nudge of the longshore current, the sting of blowing sand. Those of us who spend a lot of time on the beach can see the seasonal metamorphosis, the widening of the berm in summer, the narrowing in winter as sand is carried by storms from the beach to the offshore bars, the islands' first line of defense. But it requires all of our imagination to see the long-term adjustments of islands, their migrations, their fluidlike tendencies to roll and flow, which seem more closely related to a field of molten lava than fastland.

Imagine a satellite camera focused on the chain of barrier islands. Each month the camera clicks off a frame. Over several decades, if we join the frames to make a movie, we'll have a brief midterm view of barrier island behavior. Assuming sea level continues to rise, many of the islands will appear to roll over backward as storms dump sand leeward of the dune line, covering existing marshes and forming new beaches west of the old ones, which will become offshore bars. Some islands will appear to spin like propellers, eroding on their southern ends and accreting on the north, then reversing the process. Inlets will close and new ones will open. Islands will join together, and new islands will be formed.

On a recent trip to North Carolina's Outer Banks, we drove southward along Route 12, beginning on Knotts Island and reaching Bodie Island and Kitty Hawk shortly after noon. At lunch I remarked to a local resident that we were on a different island than the one where we had begun our trip, but I didn't recall having crossed a body of water. "Oh, the inlet between these islands closed up years ago," he said. "It's just that nobody has bothered to change the road signs and maps, because as soon as we do, the inlet will cut back through and we'll have to change the names all over again."

We spent the night at the Holiday Inn, near what used to be the inlet separating Knotts and Bodie islands. I later learned that the hotel is locally known, prophetically perhaps, as the Holiday Inlet.

If our satellite camera keeps clicking away as the next few centuries unfold, we'll have created an engrossing docudrama that includes such major characters as sea level change, glacial melt, and global warming. It's easy to see the daily, monthly, and even yearly changes in barrier island topography, but most of us still think of the larger universe as being more or less static. Of course, it is not. Changes are simply measured on a calendar with a different scale.

Over many centuries of monthly satellite photos, we'll see that not only do the islands change, but their setting changes as well. The glaciers melt and sea level rises, covering much of the land. There still will be barrier islands and salt marshes, but they will be gradually moved farther and farther west as the sea level slowly rises. One day we will reach a point when the sea level peaks and then slowly begins its ebb. Polar temperatures will climb slightly, glaciers will again rob the oceans of seawater, and the barrier beaches will begin another migration, this time eastward toward the receding sea.

It has been so for as long as anyone has been keeping score. Ice ages are not simply chapters in ancient history but part of the evolution of planet earth—a tide cycle, as it were, on a scale larger than we're used to. Instead of measuring in hours, we must think in terms of centuries or of hundreds of centuries.

In the past 1.8 million years, the sea level has risen and fallen six times. The last great low tide began its ebb about thirty-five thousand years ago and receded for more than twenty thousand years. When the tide finally began to turn, the sea level was four hundred feet lower than it is today, and the Atlantic beaches were some sixty miles east of where they are now, on the continental shelf.

Fifteen thousand years ago, huge glaciers scoured the continents, pressing north and south from the poles like invading armies, changing forever the landscapes through which they marched. In North America, the last great glacier, the Laurentide, scraped its way southward to what are now New York and New Jersey. Where the glaciers marched, the coast is rocky and rugged, scrubbed of its layer of sand and topsoil. The Laurentide Glacier drew southward as far as Long Island, whose north coast shows its rocky, glaciated past and whose south shore has the flat, sandy beaches common to the unglaciated coast.

While the coast south of New York and New Jersey was spared the last glacier, the beaches we walk upon today are glacial products, bits and pieces of the Appalachians, ground and weathered, washed into the ocean when the great ice sheets began melting twelve to fifteen thousand years ago. So our sand is indeed ancient, fragments of earth that once lay far west of us and were washed from the highlands to the sea, then lay on the seafloor for centuries more before finally being nudged back to shore by the energy of the Atlantic.

The sea level today continues to rise, as it has for the past twelve thousand years. In some future century, the high-tide portion of the cycle will again be reached, and the seas will again begin their inexorable ebb as glaciers begin to build. Of course, this is a simplified explanation of a very complex and gradual cycle. Something could happen—global warming, nuclear war—and there would be no next ice age, or it might be delayed substantially. The sea would continue to rise, and the barrier islands would continue to migrate westward, to the foothills of the Blue Ridge.

Human life, in time measured by glaciers, is less than the blink of an eye. The rise and fall of glacial tides is so gradual it seems not to occur at all, so we tend to think of the land in terms of permanence, of stability, even though it actually is shuffling slowly under our feet. The "erosion" of coastal areas is not necessarily an aberration, a symptom of something gone wrong, but evidence of another tick of the geological clock.

Perhaps the best advice for those wishing to live on the ocean could be given by the American Indians and the early European settlers, who hunted and fished on the beaches but built their homes in the safety of upland forests. There, they knew, although the sea was coming, they might at least have a good head start.

Plover Watch

The piping plover is a pit bull of a bird, a thick-necked little bully that compensates for its lack of size by being the toughest bird on the block. On Myrtle Island, as thousands of shorebirds gathered on migration stops in mid-May, we watched a solitary piping plover spend the better part of a morning pushing around a flock of larger semipalmated plovers and dunlins. With its little head held down in a butting position, it would charge the larger birds one after the other until they finally vacated the premises.

It wasn't quite clear to me why the plover was doing this. It was feeding with the other birds along the intertidal zone, well removed from its nesting area among the shell litter higher up the beach, so it wasn't necessarily a territorial dispute. Competition for food? Perhaps, but there were miles of undisturbed ocean and hundreds of acres of marine worms, sand fleas, and other plover delicacies. Besides, the piper didn't appear to be that enthusiastic about feeding. While the other plovers searched the wet sand for food, and while the dunlins dozed on one leg just outside the line of surf, the little piping plover cut a comically belligerent figure, charging one bird after another, as if in some quixotic crusade to rid itself of all potential enemies.

It seemed ironic, this little piping plover tilting at his windmills, battling imagined foes while a far more impalpable enemy whacks away at the plover's flanks. The piping plover is a beach bird, a denizen of lonely stretches of flat barrier beaches and shell piles, a bird that nests among the wracks of grass and other flotsam along the Atlantic coast and the beaches of the Great Lakes. Unfortunately for the plover, too few stretches of undisturbed beach remain, and it is falling victim to an enemy it is not equipped to fight despite its bulldoglike pugnacity. Since the turn of the century, America's beaches have been developed and manipulated at an incredible rate, and the plovers' breeding habitat has diminished accordingly.

Ornithologists believe there are two races of piping plovers, one a resident of the Great Plains, the other an eastern population that winters in the southern coastal states and in April and May travels along the coast to breeding areas from Virginia to southern Canada. Neither population is doing well. A 1990 survey showed nine hundred breeding pairs on the Atlantic coast and perhaps eight hundred more in the Great Plains. Add a small Great Lakes population, and you still have fewer than two thousand pairs remaining in North America.

No one seems to know what the piping plover population might have been fifty or one hundred years ago; nineteenth-century ornithologists apparently paid little attention to the bird, and it was not until it became apparent in the 1970s that the bird was in serious trouble that protection programs began. Currently the eastern and Great Plains populations are on the

Department of the Interior's "threatened" list, while the one hundred or so Great Lakes birds are considered endangered.

The piping plover is suffering from a severe loss of habitat, a victim of America's development of the shoreline in the last hundred years. The plovers need undeveloped beaches for nesting and food gathering, and as our inventory of undeveloped beaches has fallen, so has the number of piping plovers.

More than any other species, the piping plover symbolizes the heavy-handedness with which humans have treated the coast, and it indicates in rather indelible terms the causes and effects of changes in land use. When people move to the beaches, birds such as plovers move away. If enough people move to enough beaches, there will be none left for the plovers, and they soon will be gone.

Even before people began moving to the beaches, the piping plovers had problems enough. Understandably, the birds like to nest near their food source. On Myrtle Island they had built nesting scrapes amid the dry sand and shell fragments a few dozen feet beyond the high-tide line of the beach, a precarious situation, given the likelihood of spring northeast storms, which can push the ocean breakers up the berm of the beach and onto the shell piles where the birds nest. In a storm tide, a brood can be wiped out, forcing the birds to either nest again or wait until another season. And in addition to the tides, there is a villainous list of natural predators, ranging from fish crows and ghost crabs to raccoons.

Residential and recreational development of coastal beaches has not only taken nesting habitat from the piping plovers, but it has also created a new set of problems and predators. Fewer undeveloped beaches mean that more and more birds of various species are using the same habitat. Piping plovers are concentrated

piping plover

Wilson's plover

in increasingly smaller areas, and they must share this beach with other nesters, such as Wilson's plovers, black skimmers, and common, least, royal, Caspian, and gull-billed terns. Meanwhile, hundreds of thousands of semipalmated plovers, dunlins, red knots, sandpipers, black-bellied plovers, and ruddy turnstones gather on the beach as they make their way north to their own breeding areas in the northern provinces of Canada. Such concentrations of nesters and transients attract predators, spread disease, heighten competition for food, and add to the stress of the breeding season. Small wonder the little piping plover has such a surly personality.

While beach development has robbed the birds of habitat, it also has introduced predators normally associated with human presence: house cats, dogs, red foxes, raccoons, and opossums. Even wildlife refuges and national seashores offer little relief.

common sandpiper

semipalmated plover

About thirty pairs of piping plovers nest at Chincoteague National Wildlife Refuge on Assateague Island, which straddles the Virginia-Maryland state line. But the island has more than one million visitors a year, most of whom come during the summer beach season, when the birds are nesting and rearing their young, so protection is far from ensured, and the outlook for additional breeding sites or protected habitat is bleak.

In 1988 the Chincoteague refuge began closing a portion of the beach during the plovers' nesting season, creating a great outcry among the business leaders of the surrounding community, who feared that fewer acres of public beach would mean fewer customers for motels, campgrounds, restaurants, and gift shops. To their credit, refuge officials held firm, and the piping plovers have at least a small retreat amid a large wildlife refuge that is becoming overburdened by its human constituency.

least terns

Refuge biologists banned off-road vehicles from the plovers' nesting area and built wire enclosures to protect the birds from predators. In four years, nesting productivity increased from an average of less than 0.2 surviving chicks per nest to 1.3 chicks, a modest success but at least a reversal of a downward trend.

We walked the five miles of ocean beach on Myrtle Island, which is part of the Nature Conservancy's Virginia Coast Reserve, and counted eighteen piping plovers and ten Wilson's plovers, which are larger, darker, and more erect than the pipers. The Virginia barrier island chain is the only place on the east coast where piping and Wilson's plovers nest together. The islands are at the northern limit of the Wilson's nesting territory and at the southern limit of piping plover habitat and so provide an important sanctuary for two birds whose numbers are threatened by the same problem. With the plovers, we saw thousands of dunlins, stopping on the island to fuel up before continuing on to Canada, Alaska, and Greenland, where they would build nests in the tundra and lay their clutches of olive-colored eggs.

It's too bad, I thought, that the plovers couldn't continue northward with the dunlins, laying their eggs in the safety of the vast tundra, where the human hand has touched the earth only lightly. But the stocky little piper is not built for long-range travel; it's a commuter bird, a creature of short hops, while the dunlins are scorchers, clocked at more than one hundred miles per hour, able to fly in tight formation and to maneuver as one like a school of fish.

The plover does have a few defensive weapons in its arsenal. It's a master of camouflage, the gray-tan color of its back blending in perfectly with the sand and the shell litter in which it builds its shallow nest. When the plover crouches down and sits tight,

dunlin

willets

the bird is almost impossible to pick out amid the clutter of sun-bleached clam, oyster, and scallop shells. Even the eggs are almost impossible to find. The color of sand, spotted with black and purple, they blend almost magically into their surroundings.

It's not until the plover moves to its feeding area, where the surf breaks, that it's easily spotted. Then it stands out clearly from the darker plovers and dunlins, appearing almost white against the wet, brown sand of the surf zone. Look at it closely and you'll find a handsome little bird all dressed up in breeding plumage. A black band stretches across its breast, and another runs across the forehead, from eye to eye. The bill is orange with a black tip, and the legs and feet are also orange. In winter, when the birds return south, the black bands of breeding plumage will disappear with the molt, as will the orange on the bill and legs.

The piping plovers, like many members of the plover family, are accomplished actors. If an intruder approaches its nest, the bird will hobble off in the opposite direction, a wing extended, feigning injury. The plover will continue its act until it leads the intruder away from the nesting site; then it finally will fly off.

On Myrtle Island, six Nature Conservancy volunteers spent the day placing warning signs around the areas in which the plovers, terns, and skimmers were nesting. The project probably gave more satisfaction to us than it gave protection to the birds. At least we felt that we were doing something useful, although we realized the signs would have no effect against the most dangerous threats to this particular group: northeast storms and predators. We saw raccoon tracks near the bird colonies, and other prints that may have been made by a red fox. Ghost crabs, which kill young birds, were plentiful, as were large gulls, fish crows, and boat-tailed grackles.

The signs might keep out hikers and all-terrain-vehicle riders, but human visitors are few as the island is remote, accessible only by water. Humans usually are warned away by screeching terns and skimmers, which dive at one's head at great speed. It's difficult to imagine someone entering a bird colony and not realizing it, and yet Barry Truitt, the Conservancy's preserve manager, tells me he has found campers pitching their tents in the middle of nesting colonies, unable to figure out why the birds were raising hell with them.

The two most serious threats to the plovers—the weather and predators—are beyond the scope of even the most ambitious protection efforts. Predation has increased markedly in the years following World War II, when development of our coastal beaches began in earnest. In refuges near populated areas, house cats, dogs, raccoons, and red foxes take a large toll. On the Virginia coast, raccoons and foxes occupy most of the barrier islands, with foxes in recent years increasing in large numbers.

The piping plover perhaps is an anachronism in a world that values coastal beaches primarily as a playground for humans, a world that places a high moral value upon the life of a predator such as the red fox at the expense of an already beleaguered prey. And what if we lose the piping plover? What difference would it ultimately make if the world had one less inconspicuous little brown beach bird?

The answer, it seems to me, lies not in the survival of a single bird but what it represents in nature and in human values. The piping plover is a symbol of coastal wilderness, just as a bald eagle or a grizzly bear symbolizes the wilderness of the American West. If we lose the piping plover, we'll have lost not just a bird but a part of our history and tradition. In life the plover represents the best of the wild and the natural, and in its death it will brand us with the mark of greed, ignorance, and arrogance.

On this entire continent, less than two thousand piping plovers separate us from this final judgment. So we post our nesting-bird signs, we look out for northeast storms, we keep watch. And while we tell ourselves we do it for the birds, we know we really are doing it for ourselves.

Beachcombing

In Tom I see myself, as if I were looking at an old photograph from the family album. I stand next to our black Ford sedan while Jim, my father's English setter, nuzzles my leg. I'm wearing my Sunday suit and smiling at the camera. It must have been Easter.

I see the same smile in Tom, the innocence and trust of a six-year-old. He is experiencing what I experienced, and through him I relive my childhood. I am my father. I am my son.

Out of school, Tom spends the summer with me. In the early mornings I work as he sleeps, then he has a leisurely breakfast, watches TV, rides his bike, plays in the woods behind our house. A stick becomes a sword, a gun. His bike is a motorcycle, a truck. Our yard, so familiar, can be instantly transformed in the mind of a six-year-old to something exotic and adventurous. It is a kind of alchemy. In the half-light of the pine woods, shadows become friend and foe. I know them well.

In the afternoons we run errands—go to the post office, buy

groceries—and then we'll go out in the boat, perhaps fish for a while, go clamming, or hike the island beaches. Tom enjoys fishing if the fish are plentiful, but he prefers to be on the beach. When he is older, he will learn that part of the pleasure of fishing comes from waiting. But at six, Tom is not a good waiter. His relationship with the islands is sensual, not intellectual or contemplative. He likes the feel of coarse, wet sand on bare feet; the cold of the ocean; the power of the current; the thunderous noise of breaking surf, which is unlike any sound man can make. He likes the cries of the terns and skimmers; the discovery of jingle shells glistening at the water's edge; the delicacy of surf foam; the immensity of the ocean, sky, and beach; the thrill of being part of something wild and undefinable.

Those were my feelings, too, when my father first brought me to the islands. I must have been Tom's age. I remember most of all the power of the ocean, the wonderful thunder of crashing surf, the wildness of it all, as if we were being allowed to witness some private and intimate side of nature . . . as if we were voyeurs.

That first impression left an indelible mark on me, as I hope it will on Tom, something of a birthmark, a birthright. It would not have been the same if we had gone to a seashore resort with thousands of people, restaurants and amusement parks, hotels, boardwalks, lifeguards, and signs warning us away from the carefully built dunes. Perhaps the reason we are unwilling to preserve the last of America's wilderness beach is that we simply don't know better. Most of us are introduced to the beach at an ocean resort or, at best, a state park or national seashore, where the senses are bombarded with screaming children, pungent suntan oil, and hot asphalt. We share the beach elbow to elbow with too many near-naked strangers, each group establishing its own little community marked by a beach blanket and umbrella, intending and desiring no communication with the others. Eye contact is avoided, as if attempting to perpetuate the illusion of being alone.

As wild beaches have disappeared, more Americans have been denied the intimacy with nature—the voyeurism—that imprints upon us at an early age the wildness and power of the ocean, of the planet. At age six, tuned in to the sensual, we see beaches not as extraordinary places but as just another amusement park where we must stand in line to use the toilet.

Tom responds to the ocean by taking off his shoes, jumping out of the boat as soon as it is beached, and racing to the surf. Like a little sandpiper, he runs toward the breakers as they retreat, then races them up the berm of the beach as they come crashing in. In August his legs and back are tanned by the sun, his hair bleached nearly blond. His eyes flash as the cold water laps at his ankles, as a breaker catches him from behind.

Tom doesn't talk about the power of the ocean, the evidence it provides of the immensity and infinity of the universe. He is storing up sensual elements—sights, smells, textures, sounds—and these will over the years blend together, mixing flavors and aromas, until one day he will realize that the sum of the parts is a wonderful whole.

Forty years after I began collecting the sensual elements, I'm still trying to define them, to explain the joy that comes from being there. Perhaps now it goes beyond my sensual inventory, the sounds of the surf, the beauty of the ocean, the wild birds. It is a blend of these, yet more. It is important to be alone, I think, and to have as few reminders as possible of the nearness of civilization—that is, no roads, parking lots, boardwalks, hotels, tourists. Then I can concentrate on the real issues: the ebb and flood; the empty horizon, which requires the power of imagination to see around;

the ocean's remarkable physical power, which comes from no discernible source. Some call the experience religious, spiritual. Perhaps it is. Perhaps standing alone at the sea's edge we are close to something we cannot define or comprehend, beginning to get our feet wet.

I enjoy learning more about it. I read the field guides and scientific papers, and I talk to experts. I study coastal dynamics, watch the island birds come and go, examine grains of beach sand with a hand-held microscope bought at the local Radio Shack. These are rewarding little tasks, but they do not satisfy me completely. I store facts as if I were laying in supplies for a hurricane: flashlight, radio, extra batteries, food, water. Yet it gives me a surprisingly incomplete amount of satisfaction that I can identify the birds wading in a salt pond or can explain the workings of marsh grass.

When walking the beach, what I enjoy most is not the process of identification and cataloging but the prospect that I might stumble upon something remarkable, a spear point, perhaps, or the fossilized bone of some extinct creature, some tangible link between our time and another, a totem of sorts. Once I found the fossilized inner ear bone of a whale lying at the base of a dune, washed up by a recent storm. It looked at first like a small, misshapen human skull. Then it looked like a giant tooth. An anthropologist from the Smithsonian Institution visited a few weeks after I found the bone and identified it. He gave me a diagram of the whale skull and highlighted the inner ear bone with a yellow marker.

Twelve thousand years ago forests grew on what now is ocean floor. The barrier beaches and salt marshes were fifty or sixty miles east of here, and prehistoric creatures grazed on ancient grasses where we now fish for tuna. This tickles the imagination, to know that a northeast storm could dislodge some wonderful artifact and send it to shore.

But they are rare. Mostly we find common treasures: jingle shells, limpets, cockles, moon snails, arks, clams, scallops, and tiny snails such as wentletraps and ceriths. Jingle shells are thin, fragile, and nearly transparent. Pick up a few and put them in your pocket, and they jingle like loose change. When wet with seawater, they glitter like shiny coins. Some are white, some orange, some nearly black. They are related to razor clams, the long, thin bivalves shaped like straight razors. Tom picks them up as we walk the beach. He wants to string them together to make a decoration for the Christmas tree.

The beach, when unpaved and untrammeled by human visitors, is a busy community. In May, terns, skimmers, and plovers nest in the shell litter beyond the berm of the beach. Sea turtles lumber ashore at night and laboriously dig cavities in the sand in which they deposit dozens of leathery eggs. Predators are at work. A fish crow digs up the turtle eggs as soon as the exhausted mother disappears at dawn into the breakers. A great black-backed gull steals a tern chick. A fox raids a plover nest.

On a day in late August, Tom and I found a dead herring gull. It was an immature bird, with the smoky gray markings of youth. It had probably hatched earlier in the summer and had somehow met its demise off Metomkin Island. It could have been caught in a fisherman's net and drowned, then washed ashore. There were no visible markings indicating a violent death.

Beneath the gull a ghost crab had dug a den and was going about the process of dismantling the bird, beginning with the most accessible morsels, the eyes and brain. The crab hid in its den as we inspected the bird, no doubt wishing we would leave

mud whelks

dog whelk

moon snails

before another flood tide swept his catch back out to sea. All around the gull were the tracks of a busy ghost crab, and I could imagine him, once his den was built, circling and inspecting his great find, probing it here and there, not actually settling down to feed yet but prancing about in some sort of ghost crab wonder, thanking whatever crab deity he believed in for his great good luck.

On the beach is the beginning of life. The sea turtles that survive detection eventually hatch, and like miniature versions of their mothers plod down the berm of the beach toward the sea. The piping plovers that survive the tides, foxes, fish crows, and ghost crabs become adult birds, and in the fall they fly south. Also on the beach are other signs of success. The black egg casing of a clearnose skate has washed up. The casing has been split open and its occupant has departed, presumably to begin feeding on the small fish and shrimp of the estuary.

We find egg casings of channeled and knobbed whelks; each case, about the size of a quarter, is attached to the next by a stout membrane. Some strings of egg casings may be two feet or more in length, and each translucent compartment holds, or held, dozens of miniature whelks. The casing of the knobbed whelk has a flat edge, while the edge of the channeled whelk casing is sharp. Now and then, if you slice open a casing with a knife, you can find a few tiny whelk shells inside, homes of the few animals that did not make it. But mostly the casings are filled with sand, which they picked up while tumbling around in the surf.

At summer's end our back porch is filled with island treasures. We have dozens of limpets, fascinating little shells in gray or orange that look like miniature volcanoes. We have bits of coral and lacy little stones that actually are colonies of tiny animals

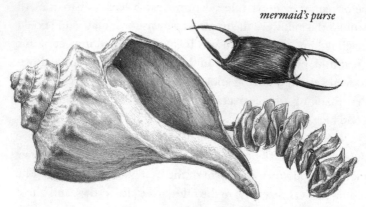

mermaid's purse

channeled whelk and egg casings

called bryozoans, which often build their communities around a pebble or shell. Large clam shells or the shells of sea scallops are put to use in the kitchen as individual serving dishes for deviled crab or clam. I collect a few large ark shells for a friend who carves wooden decoys. Arks have well-defined ribs, which my friend uses to paint the vermiculated feather detail on the sides of duck decoys. He dabs the shell in paint, then presses it onto the wooden carving, transposing a likeness of feathers. There are sand dollars; the purple-specked shells of lady crabs; an unidentified fossilized bone, possibly a shark vertebra; and the jagged tail of a horseshoe crab. It is an eclectic and totally worthless collection, valuable only for the reminders it provides of the beach.

The charm of a wilderness beach lies not in what is there, but in the promise of what it might yield on the next trip or in what might lie around that next set of dunes. The value of an island wilderness is not measured by the known, but by the unknown.

The real worth of wilderness is that it keeps alive the six-year-old in us; it demands imagination, curiosity, faith, trust, and a childlike ability to see beyond the horizon.

In an ancient and fossilized oyster shell, much larger than those currently growing in the marsh, we have a link with that world now covered by the sea and separated from us by some twelve thousand years. The oyster grew in the Pleistocene marshes and fed some hunter-gatherer who plucked it from a cluster of shells, chipped its edge with a stone, and sucked out its salty meat and juices. He lived somewhere off the present coast, building fires in an ancient forest long flooded, scavenging the marshes and beaches as I do today, prying clams from the mud for his dinner. I wonder what he thought as he walked along the beach. With his belly full of oyster meat, did he look to the ocean, at the horizon curving away, and wonder?

People who have lived along the coast tend to be religious. Perhaps it has something to do with our nearness to the unknown, the constant reminders of the infinity of the universe, the presence of powers beyond our control. To survive, we must have faith. We must believe that the tides will flood only so far, and then they will ebb. It is high water at noon today, and by six this evening it will be low. Tomorrow, the cycle will advance by about forty minutes. We know the truth of tides, and we live to their rhythms, although we can do nothing to alter the ebb and flood, which is connected to the spin of the earth, the orbit of the moon, barometric pressure, the mysterious push and pull of unseen powers. Yet the process is precise and predictable; those of us who live on the coast stake our lives on it.

Storms often push the tides higher than normal, flooding low areas of mainland, but such occurrences are business as usual for the estuarine system. A northeaster, for example, blows the water toward the land while the moon's gravity pulls it, building tides higher than normal. Water becomes "stacked up" in the salt marsh creeks because the wind pushes it in during flood tide and hampers its departure as the tide ebbs. But still the tide will turn at approximately the appointed hour, and although it might not recede as much as usual, it will eventually recede.

We trust implicitly in the tidal cycles, planning our fishing and clamming trips to coincide with the period of tide that gives us the best advantage, even choosing our homesites just beyond the reach of the highest tides. We seldom stop to comprehend the efficiency and dependability of the phenomenon. What if one day it were to fail? What if one day the tide neglected to ebb and instead reached the point of high tide and continued to rise, pressing landward for another six hours, and another six after that? If the average tidal change is five feet, then by missing a single ebb cycle, the tide would rise ten feet above mean high water. The result would be catastrophic. In populated areas, businesses, homes, and schools would be flooded, damage would be in the millions, and there would be loss of life. In rural areas, fertile farmland and forests would be poisoned by salt water, waterfront villages inundated, boats torn from their moorings, docks and piers uprooted, and inlets and channels resculpted. A single lapse in the mechanics of tidal change would devastate the landscape, at least temporarily, and it would destroy our faith in the powers of the coastal system. Families would pack their station wagons and head for Nebraska. Great bargains would be found in waterfront property.

So strong is our faith in the immutability of the tides that we gather by the millions just out of harm's way, building our homes, playgrounds, offices, and schools just beyond the longest lick of high water. Building on the ocean beach, however, has more to do with foolishness than faith. While the process of ebb and flood is dependable, its exactness is cushioned by a margin of storms and other atmospheric conditions that blur the precision of the tide tables. While the ebb and flood are dependable, nature sometimes adds surprises.

The surprises, I think, are important. On the beach, we sense a nearness to a force of great power and mystery. It is as if we were testing a sleeping giant, tickling his feet as he slumbers. A northeast storm, or the approach of a hurricane, excites us in a peculiar way, and although we acknowledge the danger, we are somehow drawn to it, as if being allowed to witness one of nature's more intimate moments, a rare opportunity to become voyeurs once again.

While studying the barrier islands and salt marshes provides evidence of things seen, I think it is important also to experience the islands on a different level, and this can be done in a wilderness setting, where the distractions are kept to a minimum. The most important discoveries we make are those not found in field guides and scientific literature. Like belief in the supernatural, the islands force us to use our imagination to see beyond the horizon, to see beyond the barrier of years to a world that once existed here and that someday will return. Like religion, the islands require child-like innocence. The power of the ocean thrills us, frightens us, and feeds and nurtures us.

To find and identify a shell or a bird is satisfying because in a small way it helps us to comprehend this vast interlocking system of ocean, beaches, dunes, marshes, bays, and mainland. Yet the most compelling aspect of the islands lies not in the things we find and identify, but in those not yet found, in that which lies beyond the horizon. The possibilities, when imagined, are without limit. It is not until they are described and identified that the limits are enforced.

I think Tom senses this as he races into the surf, feeling the cold, powerful breakers crash around him and pull at him. He knows he's at the edge of something remarkable, and he doesn't know what it is. That, as I remember, is how I felt when my father first took me to the islands.

Small Boats

One can never have too many boats. At last count, four were parked in our yard: the sixteen-foot outboard we use for fishing and general running around; a sixteen-foot canoe; a small, lightweight, one-person canoe; and a little eleven-foot kayak that's perfect for exploring the upper reaches of the marsh.

Our boat collection is not complete, and it never will be, as it is subject to constant change. Someday I'd like to have a bigger boat, something with a little cabin, that can be used to explore the Chesapeake Bay or to chase down schools of bluefish in Tangier Sound. I'd like a sea kayak to use on the shallow seaside bays. And I need a small, stable skiff with a seven-horse kicker for marsh henning. This may sound like an extravagant fleet for one man to own, but when you spend a lot of time on the water, you discover that boats are like shoes: Different styles are made for different functions.

The sixteen-foot outboard is too big and heavy for marsh henning, it's too noisy for quiet explorations up shallow creeks, and it's too small for trips in the open Chesapeake. It's a good seaside boat, perfect for quickly getting out to the barrier islands, for flounder fishing, for clamming, for bird-watching in the marsh.

But I spend most of my time on the water in small boats—the big canoe if I have a partner, the kayak or small canoe if I'm alone. You cannot have too many boats, and the best boat for a given situation is the smallest one that will accomplish the task safely and with comfort. The outboard is good transportation: It gets me to the islands or fishing areas quickly, and should a storm develop, I can be back at the dock in a matter of minutes. But experiencing the marsh in an outboard is like flying over Montana at forty thousand feet and saying you've visited grizzly country. An outboard, because of its size, speed, and noise, is an intrusion. If all you need is to go from the dock to the clamming flats, then the outboard is fine, but if you want to get to know the marsh, you should have as little as possible between you and the elements.

The little kayak weighs about forty pounds, including its double-bladed paddle, has flotation in bow and stern for safety, and is remarkably stable. We play around with it at the beach in summer, and it takes an effort to capsize it. The kayak sits low in the water. A molded plastic seat is only an inch or two off the bottom of the boat, and a swiveling seat back makes paddling a comfort. A spray skirt came with the kayak. You slip it over your head and shoulders like a sweater, then fit the elastic bottom around a rim that encircles the cockpit. With the spray skirt on, you can paddle in choppy water without getting wet, and it prevents water from running down the paddle and dripping into your lap, which is a nice feature for winter trips.

A small boat puts you down near water level, eye to eye with the water birds, and it lets you feel the pull of the current, as if you were part of the stream and belonged there. The best way to explore the marsh is to remove as many of the barriers as you can that prevent you from seeing, hearing, smelling, and feeling the various elements of the marsh. You could, of course, simply pull off your boots and wade in, but in most marshes this is seldom practical. The canoe or kayak is just about right. It doesn't intrude, and it is responsive to the current and to the paddle. In a small boat, propelled by paddle instead of internal combustion, you're in control.

Birds don't seem to fear canoes and kayaks. Perhaps it's the low center of gravity, the sleek profile, the quiet way the boat cuts through water. I paddled up Folly Creek recently and wedged the canoe under a myrtle thicket to have lunch. The thicket was full of yellow-rumped warblers, which were feasting on the blue berries of the myrtle bushes. I ate my ham sandwich and they ate their berries; we were only a few feet apart.

The myrtle thicket where I shared lunch with the warblers borders a farm field where I often hunt quail or, when the season is out, go hiking. I walked the farm the week after going canoeing, and the yellow-rumps were still in the myrtle bushes, but they would let me approach only to within about thirty feet before flitting off to the next thicket. Even when they stayed put they were on constant alert, keeping an eye on me rather than fueling up with myrtle berries.

The marsh creeks that separate the barrier islands from the mainland typically are bordered by cordgrass (*Spartina alterniflora*), but as they join the land, the water becomes brackish and the cordgrass gives way to needlerush, fleabane, sedge, cattail, and, on higher ground, thickets of myrtle, greenbrier, cedar, sweet gum, and oak, which in our rural setting usually separate the creek from a farm field. Most of the upland birds using that particular field are found in this edge habitat, the narrow fringe of hardwoods and dense understory that separates the field from the marsh. Here in this narrow thicket, they have protection from predators, plentiful and varied sources of food, and adequate places to nest and rest. In habitat like this, birds expect danger to come from land, in the form of humans or foxes, or from overhead, as in Cooper's and red-tailed hawks. Birds seldom expect danger to come from the creekside and are less wary of strangers paddling canoes.

I normally put in along the wider portions of a stream and then paddle toward the headwaters. If it's a tidal creek, I time the trip to take advantage of the rising tide as I paddle up the creek, and then I return as the tide ebbs.

On the northern shore of Folly Creek is a farm owned by the Nature Conservancy. During the 1930s it was a popular golf course, but the greens have long since been plowed under and the fairways are planted in soybeans and tomatoes. The only reminder of the golf course is at the site of the old clubhouse, where a few remaining foundation bricks and tumbled-down storage buildings on a small bluff overlook the creek. Boats used to dock here, and a very narrow marsh separates the fastland from the water. It's a good place to launch a canoe. I drive the truck down to the creek edge, lift the canoe off the rack, and slide it through the wispy marsh grass toward deeper water.

I like most of all the first few moments of a canoe trip, when you leave land and glide through water, testing the balance of the boat, getting the feel of things. It's like being weightless. You look up and see the sky, and you look down and see the sky reflected in the water. You're floating, and only a gentle wake defines the margin of air and water. It's a pleasure to leave land

and its firmness; to glide through water seems so effortless—one pull on the paddle and away you go. The transformation is sudden, and it is a delight.

Winter is the best time. I put in at the old golf club and paddle up the creek, which quickly narrows and becomes brackish. In winter the water is clear, free of the phytoplankton, zooplankton, and other flotsam that cloud the shallow streams during warm weather. I look down and watch the bottom roll by. There are logs, dead branches, long grasses floating in the current, even in winter.

Indians once lived here. Long before there was golf, they hunted along the creekbank, spearing fish, gathering oysters, snaring black ducks. These were the Metomkins, one of the local tribes that resisted the encroachment of whites, to no avail. I have found shell middens in the woods and fields, remains of camps and villages where Metomkin men, women, and children gathered around campfires, roasting oysters and making plans for hunts. Little could they have known that people would one day play golf here, and then grow tomatoes, and then go exploring in small boats, finding their bleached oyster shells and wondering what their lives might have been like. Did they kneel here as I do and watch the ducks gather? Did they pray to whatever god they believed in to help them fill their bellies?

I glide along the creek and watch the bottom pass by, half expecting to find something significant down there. A stone axe, perhaps, or a spear point. But there are only broken branches washed down by storm tides, and yellow grasses whipping about in the silent storm of the current.

The creek narrows and branches off in several directions, each stream part of a watershed, draining the mainland all the way back to the subtle ridge that runs along the center of the peninsula. Everything on the eastern side of the ridge drains toward the ocean, and everything on the western side drains toward the Chesapeake Bay. It's a complex vascular network of veins and arteries, with the pulse of tides pushing water through creeks, bays, guts, and ditches, ebbing and flooding with comforting regularity. The ocean, barrier islands, salt marshes, bays, and creeks form a single organism, a massive and complex estuarine system that shares the same blood. Even when paddling a small canoe in a small, brackish stream far inland, you can feel the pulse.

I round a bend and surprise half a dozen black ducks. They were snoozing in the marsh, sipping fresh water flowing down the watershed stream toward the ocean. At first they went on alert, heads high, and then they were gone, leaving small ripples in the shallow water. Ducks enjoy these little freshets, where rainwater flows from the towns and villages, from farm fields and residential lawns, to become part of the salt marsh estuary. When paddling up a creek toward the headwaters, you suddenly realize that the flow is no longer governed by the tides, but by freshwater runoff, the product of the watersheds. The demarcation line between tidal creek and watershed is negotiable, depending upon the amount of recent rainfall and the tidal cycle. During dry weather, a high tide can reach far up the creek, pushing salt water far inland. But during periods of heavy rain, the salinity of the water in the creeks drops, sometimes threatening oysters and other sessile animals that prefer daily infusions of salt water.

In less than half a mile, the character of the creek changes from salty to brackish to fresh. As salinity changes, so do the communities of plants, animals, and birds. Saltwater plants such as *Spartina alterniflora*, *Spartina patens*, and *Salicornia* give way to black needlerush, a coarse grass with sharp stems that turn

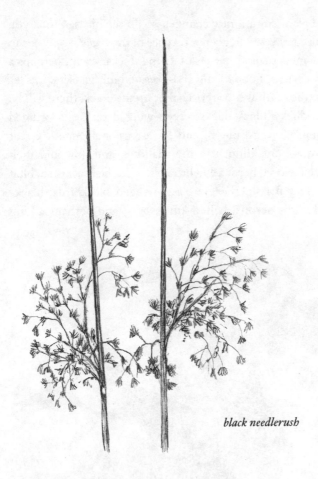

black needlerush

dark gray or black in winter; sea oxeye, a low shrub with thick, succulent leaves and brilliant yellow flowers that become brown, burlike seed heads in winter; fleabane; rose mallow, or marsh hibiscus, which has large pink or white blossoms in summer; cattail; and pickerelweed, a common intertidal-zone plant with huge, heart-shaped leaves and blue flower spikes.

As the plant community changes, so do the birds. When you paddle along the wider, deeper reaches of the creek, you'll see in fall and winter several species of diving ducks: scaup, perhaps a few canvasbacks, hooded and red-breasted mergansers, buffleheads. In the shallower waters farther up the creek, there will be dabbling ducks: black ducks, green-winged teal, blue-winged teal, mallards, wood ducks, and the occasional pintail. Great blue herons hunt killifish in the shallows, and now and then we'll see tricolored herons and little blues. In the brackish habitat of the upper marsh, there are red-winged blackbirds, black-crowned night herons, belted kingfishers, and perhaps a king

pintails

wood ducks

mallard

rail. Northern harriers will patrol the marsh and adjacent fields, and we'll usually see a red-tailed hawk or two soaring overhead.

Throughout the creek there will be laughing gulls and herring gulls in summer, ring-billed gulls in winter. We can count on least, common, and Forster's terns. We'll see cormorants, ospreys, yellowlegs, whimbrels, skimmers, willets, glossy ibises, clapper rails, boat-tailed grackles, and oystercatchers.

In the upper reaches of a tidal creek, where marsh grass brushes the boat on both sides and the trees begin to close in, you're likely to see most anything. Within the space of a few dozen feet, you might jump a pair of black ducks, disturb a sleeping great horned owl, launch a great blue heron, put up a covey of quail, watch a harrier catch a field mouse, see a kingfisher hover and dive, or spot in the underbrush brown thrashers, American robins, mockingbirds, a variety of sparrows, marsh wrens, and thrushes.

It's a remarkable zone, this transition area between salt marsh and upland, where an hour of paddling a canoe can take you from the regimentation of the salt marsh proper and *Spartina alterniflora* to tiny freshets that wind through woods and fields.

In a canoe, these worlds are separated only by a few strokes of the paddle, but biologically they are separate entities connected by a common element—water—yet each assigned its specific territory, each its own character, each element blending to create a wonderful and diverse whole.

Salted Fish

Last week we said goodbye to summer. It was a brilliant fall day, beginning with a frosty morning but warming to T-shirt weather by noon. It began with a prelude to winter and ended with a reminder of summer, a delicious mix for a late-season fisherman, but a very temporary one. Fishing in October is like taking the last of the candy from the bowl.

We said goodbye to summer by catching spot, a few small gray trout, and some sea bass, then we cleaned them thoroughly and packed them away in twenty-five pounds of salt in an old stone crock.

Come January, we'll roll out of bed one dark and rainy Sunday morning, put a few of the salty fillets in boiling water, fry a few thick slices of country bacon, scramble some eggs, make some biscuits, and pop open a fresh jar of fig preserves. We'll taste again that sweet October fishing day.

My great-grandparents salted fish because they had to. They had no freezers in those days, so in October the trout, croakers, and spot went into the old stone crocks, covered with a snowy blanket of salt. From Thanksgiving until Easter, the family ate salted fish.

By February, I would imagine, salted fish would have become a fairly tiresome source of protein. With each salty bite, they would count the days until the first flounder of spring would arrive, providing fresh seafood for the table.

I'm sure we enjoy salted fish much more than they did, simply because we choose to eat them. It's not a matter of survival with us, but it does make me feel that I'm prepared for winter, now that the old stone crock is filled.

Beneath the cloth cover, the fresh fish and the salt are going about their chemical reaction, a marriage of earth and sea, holding in suspension the last of summer as we await a new spring.

I suppose I enjoy the tradition of salting fish as much as I enjoy eating them. It's a practice that links the generations, one that is virtually unchanged since the colonists arrived. Our old stone crock has been used for so many years for salting fish that the salt has leached through the glazing and into the clay. No matter how many times you wash it, a white filigree of salt will decorate the dark inner walls of the container as soon as it dries.

I prepare the fish by scaling and filleting them and washing them thoroughly in fresh water to remove all traces of blood, which could cause the fish to spoil. Then I pack them in salt in the old crock. A layer of salt, a layer of fillets. And so on until I run out of fillets.

All that remains is for the fish to make a brine and then to wait for a sufficiently raw Sunday morning on which to enjoy them for breakfast.

For salting, fish must go without delay from the island estuary

to the salt crock. A day or so in a seafood market refrigerator and they are useless. The process depends upon salt reacting with the moisture in the tissues of the fish to make a brine, and once taken from the sea, fish dehydrate quickly. When salted while they are very fresh, the meat will stay firm and white throughout the winter. If the fish are allowed to dehydrate before salting, you'll have a crock of yellow, leathery fillets more suitable for shoemaking than Christmas breakfast.

For that reason, it pays to catch your own or to purchase your fish directly from a local waterman. In the early fall we'll buy a bag of salt and clean the stone crock, anticipating a productive fishing trip. That way we're ready. As soon as we return from a

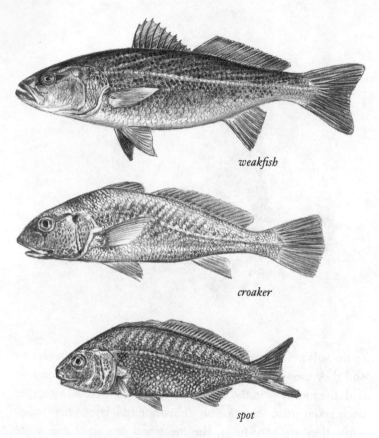

weakfish

croaker

spot

good day on the water, we'll clean the fish and salt them away before taking care of the other post-trip chores, such as washing the boat and stowing the fishing tackle.

We prefer to salt small fillets of gray trout, croaker, or spot, which usually linger into the fall on the Virginia coast. This year we caught a few sea bass, so I filleted them and added them to the crock. I've never salted sea bass, but the firm, white meat looks like it should do well. Neither have I salted freshwater fish such as bass and bluegill, although I guess they would salt as nicely as the trout and spot.

In our health-conscious world, consuming salted fish regularly is considered as risky as Russian roulette. My grandparents and great-grandparents ate them regularly to supplement their steady diet of salted hams, shoulders, and sidemeat from the smokehouse, as well as eggs, sausage, scrapple, bacon, and other high-fat foods. Although they lived well into their eighties, they worked on a small family farm and did not stop working long enough during the day to allow fat to accumulate. Our lifestyle is different, and salted fish is the occasional treat—the taste of tradition—not the staple it once was for earlier generations.

Ironically, the first Virginia barrier island settled by English explorers was claimed because of its salt-making capacity and its nearness to fish and wild game. Capt. Samuel Argall, exploring the area in 1613, reported to the acting governor of Virginia, Sir Thomas Dale, that the waters of the Virginia barrier islands held a "great store of fish, both shell-fish and other." The only problem was that the great store of fish, as well as waterfowl and game animals, would not keep for long unless preserved in brine. Thus the great store of fish would be of little value unless they could be preserved for a reasonable length of time.

Argall reasoned that salt could be boiled from seawater on nearby Smith Island, the southernmost in the chain, only a brief sailing trip from the Jamestown colony. So a company of men was dispatched to the island to build great vats in which to boil seawater and extract salt.

Years later, on nearby Mockhorn Island, an interior island with little high land, evaporation ponds were built to extract salt from seawater in what might have been America's first solar-powered industry. According to Ralph T. Whitelaw's *Virginia's*

Eastern Shore, John Custis, the great-grandfather of Martha Custis Washington, entered into a contract with Peter Reverdy on April 4, 1668, to make salt on the island, which was then owned by Custis. Reverdy was apparently an expert at the salt-making process, and a lengthy contract gave him instructions to build 312 clay-lined evaporation ponds for extracting salt from seawater.

Whitelaw doesn't report on the fate of the business venture, but the lengthy contract, the involvement of a salt-making professional, and the very scope of the project are evidence of the importance of salt in the lives of the early residents of the Virginia coast.

I feel somewhat ashamed that I bought my twenty-five pounds of salt for a modest sum at the local market. Today we take salt for granted and even avoid it when possible. But these are special times, and the salting of fish is more a religious act than a means of warding off winter famine. I drove to the market in my car, and I am writing these words on a word processor, in a room cooled and heated by a heat pump.

While I make no salt, cut and split very little wood, and seldom depend upon my legs to take me significant distances, I'm not so sure my life is that much better than that of my great-grandparents. They took for granted a world that we seem desperately trying to hold in our grasp. In their day, it seemed there would forever be a great store of fish, swimming in clean waters from Maine to Florida. Today the salt is easy to come by and the fish are precious.

Teal

A flock of green-winged teal sounds from a distance like a choir of spring peepers on a warm March night. We heard them long before we saw them. They were at the head of the creek feeding on the wide, shallow flats, stirring about in the soft mud for seeds and crustaceans, whistling as they worked.

We were about two hundred yards away, separated from the birds by a thick pine woods. Had it been twenty degrees warmer, we might indeed have mistaken the teal for peepers, but with the temperature hovering near the freezing mark, no frog in its right mind would be celebrating spring. Besides, now and then we would hear the guttural cackle of a hen, and the black ducks would occasionally let rip with a strident quack.

The idea was to stalk the birds, to get as close as we could without frightening them. The duck season had ended weeks ago, and we were armed with binoculars, although I was wishing I had brought the camera as well. We walked quietly through the woods, and then, as we approached the myrtle thicket that separates the marsh from the upland woods, we crawled.

Tom thought it was a great adventure, and he soon learned to avoid the greenbrier thickets. The necessity of remaining absolutely quiet for an extended period of time was a tough assignment, but he held up fairly well, with only a few brief lapses.

We crawled through the myrtles, taking note of the rich fragrance of bay leaves, and soon we descended a gentle slope and for the first time saw the ducks through an opening in the thicket. Hundreds of waterfowl were congregated at the creek head, mainly green-winged teal, but also several dozen black ducks, a few mallards, and some hooded mergansers and buffle-heads, which stood out clearly from the others. The drakes were formal looking in their black and white plumage, and the hens were sleek and stylish. Their fanned-out crests, when backlit by the sun, looked like halos.

We wanted to get even closer, so we slid on our backs along the carpet of pine shatters until we reached the edge of the woods and the beginning of the marsh. The ducks feeding along our side of the creek sensed something was wrong, and, with heads held high and alert, they swam to the opposite shore.

Tom and I settled down beneath a large pine tree. I leaned against it, and he sat in my lap as we took turns with the binoculars. Our spot was ideal. Myrtles hid us on both sides, but we had a clear view of the creek in front of us through the undergrowth. The sun broke through the canopy and warmed us as we sat against the pine.

As we waited for the ducks to resume their business, I began counting the teal, finally giving up at two hundred, with many more uncounted beyond the bend in the creek and up little guts in the marsh. It was the largest concentration of teal I had seen,

green-winged teal

and there were close to fifty black ducks with them. Blacks are large ducks anyway, but when measured on a teal scale they look like geese. I saw one standing erect on the far shore and thought at first it was a heron.

After twenty minutes or so, the teal resumed feeding and whistling and then swam back to our side of the creek. We sat motionless, watching them through the binoculars. Soon they were right under our bank, no more than twenty yards away.

The teal drake is a handsome little bird, not nearly as gaudy as the drake wood duck, but no less resplendent. Its breast is the color of champagne, overlaid with random brown dots. In the subspecies we have here in Virginia the breast is separated from the gray, vermiculated sides by a bold white line. The head is a reddish chestnut color, with a wide, metallic green stripe beginning behind the eye and extending down the neck. The green stripe is spectacular when the sun hits it. On some of the birds we watched, it appeared bright blue when the sun was at a sharp angle.

Tom had scarcely moved since we took our position under the big pine, and I thought that he, too, had been caught up in the comings and goings of the teal. I congratulated him on being so quiet, but he did not respond. Lying there on the soft pine carpet, warmed by the winter sun, he was asleep.

December Light

C all it Christmas. Here we are in mid-December and the temperature is in the sixties. The sky is blue. The breeze is gentle. The tide is high.

I load the little canoe into the truck and drive down to the farm. I have the binoculars, a sponge for sopping up water dropped from the paddle, a flotation vest, and both the double-bladed paddle and a single blade. The double is for the wide water where I put in, and the single is for maneuvering where the creek narrows down and begins snaking its way toward land.

It's a day worth saving. Such days are rare in December. It has been cold, and it will be colder soon, and the cold will last a long time. In a month the little creek will have ice on it; it may even be frozen over. But today the surface of the water is summertime flat, with barely a ripple. I slide the canoe through the marsh grass and feel the bow take float, then I push the stern in, standing on grass tumps to keep my feet dry. I step over the stern, stay low and centered in the boat, and make my way forward to the single seat. I thrust my weight forward several times, and the canoe slides through the grass and then floats freely. I settle in, balance the double-bladed paddle on the gunwales, take the lens caps off the binoculars, and put the binoculars around my neck. I kick off my shoes and get comfortable.

The tide is still rising slightly, and it's an easy paddle toward the head of the Folly Creek. It feels good being on the open water in the little boat. It's about twelve feet long and weighs less than thirty-five pounds, which makes it about as portable as a boat can get. I can drive it down woods roads in the truck, hang it over my shoulder, and hike down to the water with the paddle and PFD lashed to the center thwart. It's a great way to explore the upper reaches of tidal creeks, which normally are too shallow for motor boats but too mucky for walking. I can slide the boat in and within minutes leave civilization behind.

Here on the upper creeks, where the cordgrass begins to close in on open water, it's easy to imagine you're the first human visitor since . . . who? Some Metomkin hunter-gatherer trapping muskrats? Incredibly, with so much great canoeing water on the Eastern Shore peninsula, few people own canoes. If I stop at the shopping center to buy some snacks on my way to the farm, someone is inevitably inspecting the canoe in the back of the truck when I come out of the store. "How do you know which end's her bow and which end's her stern?" he or she will ask.

I was paddling on Finney Creek recently, and two men were fishing their fatback nets along a shoal area near the mouth of the creek. The man in the bow greeted me with a laugh. "I told Ed that if we put her aground it'll be the first time we've ever been pulled off by a canoe," he said.

The canoe is a boat made for the senses. I paddle out to the middle of the wide water and just sit there, listening, watching. I hear a dog barking in the distance, then the soft, busy whistle of yellow-rumped warblers feeding in a myrtle thicket on the shore. I hear a familiar whistle, look up, and an osprey glides over. Its head is pointed downward and it is reading the water, looking for the quick shadow of a mullet. I remain still, and I don't think it even sees me. Or if it does it pays me no mind. It's awfully late in the year for an osprey to be around, I think.

In winter, the water is clear, free of the plankton and other microscopic plants and animals that cloud the shallows. I look down and see oysters glide by, their shells surprisingly white against the dark of the bottom. There is dead grass down there, matted with mud and debris, rotting slowly as it passes its stored energy to the marsh world. As the water warms, bacteria will begin munching and the grass will be reduced to an assortment of molecules, each of which will pass its energy, captured from the sun of last summer, to billions of animals too small to see. And they in turn will pass the energy to larger animals, and eventually the molecules will again become part of the grasses, part of the oysters and clams.

The arrangement seems simple and efficient, and I think that when I die I would like to become part of the salt marsh estuary. Scatter my ashes over the marsh and the creek water, and put my old body back in circulation. Don't put me in an expensive satin-lined box and drop the box into a concrete vault six feet under. No, I'd rather be returned to these waters, to the grasses and the phytoplankton, where there is no such thing as death, only the cycles of life. Make my marker a lush stand of cordgrass. Watch it wave in the breeze, observe how it catches the light of fall, and think of me.

The light is spectacular on this December morning. There is a richness, an increase in resolution, as if our vision has suddenly been enhanced. We see colors with more saturation. The grass and trees have more detail. A kingfisher perched on a pine limb is resplendent with her blue-gray crest, white throat, and rusty flanks and belly band. She chatters loudly in protest as I glide under her, then flies off to search for killifish at the creek head.

That, too, is where I'm headed. As the creek narrows, I enjoy the increased sensation of speed. The grass along the bank whizzes by, and I like the quiet, quick movement of the boat, propelled only by my arms, shoulders, legs, and the plastic paddle. I enjoy the feeling of my muscles at work, propelling me, and I enjoy, too, the control I can exert on my movements. I switch to the single-blade paddle as the creek begins to narrow down and wind through the marsh. A J-stroke takes me quickly around a bend without touching the grass on the bank. I'm careful not to rattle the paddle against the side of the canoe; to do so would spook any wildlife that might wait around the next bend, and it would also be bad form. For a few minutes I enjoy paddling as quickly as I can, executing the proper strokes, making all the turns, and doing it quietly. The only sound is the pulling of water, the resistance of the still water to a moving boat, the drip and spray of water from the paddle. I feather the paddle on the return stroke, scarcely bringing it out of the water, allowing the blade to slice through air and water before I turn it at the last split second and pull water, sending the little canoe into the next turn. The feeling is like that of sailing a small boat, when you use all the elements available to you and all the technique you know to wrest the highest level of performance from the craft. But the reward in canoeing is not just the sense of speed, but knowing that I am doing this by myself, with no engines or sails to help me. I am in control.

Suddenly there is an explosion. The water erupts in front of me, and the still air is beaten by two dozen wings. Black ducks. I surprised them as I rounded a bend, and they shook me out of my reverie. I don't think I have ever gotten so close to black ducks; I can feel their spray and hear the muffled strength of their wingbeats. One or two seem frozen in profile, heads extended, feet dangling, wings cupping air. The sun glints on their metallic blue speculums, and their gray underwings appear pure white. I can look them in the eye and for an instant see their surprise and fright, their wildness. Just as quickly, they are gone.

I sit in the canoe and breathe deeply, watching the ducks fly farther back into the marsh. I used to hunt black ducks some years ago, when there were more of them and when I was younger. In those days I'd have longed for such an experience— a close-range covey rise of black ducks. And I wondered now, if I had carried a shotgun, whether I could have pulled the trigger. A part of me says yes. I enjoyed the sight and the sound of the flush, the head-clearing jolt of wingbeats all around me. How great it would be now to taste that wildness, that rich flavor of duck breast, which would bring back the sensations I felt when the ducks jumped.

Yet the life of these birds seems too precious to waste, too fleeting and temporary. Perhaps they will reward someone else with the same experience they gave to me, or perhaps I may share the marsh with them again. Death would end these possibilities. Would I value the experience any less for having ended it with the birds flying off? Or is the taste of duck breast the proper end to such an encounter? I honestly don't know. I do know I've had my taste of wild duck, perhaps enough to last me. I didn't miss the shotgun.

Slow down, I tell myself. This is not a race. Enjoy the day, enjoy the light.

I do like the look of fall light on marsh grass, especially in the upper marsh where thick stands of saltmeadow hay, *Spartina patens*, lie in cowlicks under cedars and marsh elders. The tide seldom reaches the stands of saltmeadow hay, so the previous season's crop of grass is not washed into the estuary as it is with *Spartina alterniflora*. Instead, *Spartina patens* collapses where it stands and gradually decomposes in the same cowlick configuration in which it grew. You can run your hand under the current crop, gently pull it back, and see last year's stand, its cowlick spiraling in a different direction. If you're careful, you can pull away the two-year-old growth and see the remains of a third year's crop.

Jump up and down and the marsh will shudder underfoot. You're walking on soft mud, but with a tough crust of decaying *Spartina patens* on top, the fine blades interlocking to form a springboard.

It's best to visit such a marsh in the fall and winter, when the grass turns deep brown and the low sun sidelights it, bringing out all the texture of the layers of grass. Find a stand with some black needlerush, and you'll have a nice yin and yang salt marsh landscape. *Spartina patens* is a feminine plant, soft, fine, gently curved, pliant. Needlerush is straight, rigid, strong, unyielding. In December the sharp stalks turn black, providing a counterpoint to the gentle saltmeadow hay in color, texture, and character.

A *Spartina patens* marsh retains its beauty year-round. In spring it will suddenly, magically, turn from brown to emerald green, last year's cowlicks yielding to fresh growth. *Spartina alterniflora*, however, gets messy in winter. I canoe through the tidal marsh, and on both sides of the narrow creek the grass is still tall, but brown. Only a few inches of green remain near the roots. In another month the remaining tall blades will be sheared off by ice, beaten down by wind and tide, smothered by snow. The life of the plant will retreat to the rhizomes, until the first warm days of spring send forth new shoots and the cycle begins again.

The creek narrows and the marsh becomes brackish. Actually, it no longer is a creek, but a gut, or perhaps a drain (pronounced *dreen*). In the taxonomy of bodies of water on the seaside, a creek is a wide, navigable tidal passage. A gut is smaller and is navigable only by small boats. A drain is smaller still, sort of a ditch, but not manmade.

Folly Creek, like most seaside creeks, does not simply end. It narrows to a gut, then to a drain, then disappears into a greenbrier thicket in a pine woods. At that point it is part of the watershed, draining land all the way back to the town of Accomac, three or four miles away. Yellow signs are placed along the creek bank warning against the consumption of shellfish taken from the upper portions of the creek. This is because the health department has found high levels of fecal coliform bacteria in the water, the product of nonfunctioning or nonexistent septic systems in the town. These are sobering reminders, these yellow signs. While the creek may appear wild and timeless with its black ducks and kingfishers, we know that the life of the creek is affected by events taking place miles away, far beyond the grove of pines and greenbrier into which the creek disappears.

When I can make no further progress, I paddle backward until I find a spot wide enough to turn the canoe around. The old duck hunter in me makes note that this would be a fine spot

great blue heron and Spartina *grass*

for black ducks and teal. The water is shallow and fresh, and at high tide the ducks would come here to eat, drink, and rest, especially if the weather was bad. There is a little mound on the north side of the creek, covered with shrubs. I could put out ten or twelve decoys, stash the canoe behind the mound, hunker down in the shrubs, and get some fine shooting. The morning sun would be behind me. I wouldn't even need a blind.

But I somehow know I'll never hunt the spot. There is a one-bird limit on black ducks, and it would hardly be worth the trouble of paddling up here before dawn, setting out the decoys, and then having the day end with the first bird bagged. But I know, too, that's not the real reason I'll not hunt here. It's more complicated than that.

I paddle back to the wide part of the creek at an easy pace. Now and then a pair of black ducks will fly over, get a look at me, and change direction. I see teal back in the marsh ponds. Occasionally a flock of twenty or more will get up, fly across the marsh in a pack like dunlins, then drop back into the grass. I surprise a great blue heron as he fishes along the creek edge; he leaves with a raucous squawk that sounds like a chain saw with carburetor problems.

My arms and shoulders are tired, my right leg is numb from sitting for too long on the wooden seat. I stop paddling, lie back against the deck, stretch my legs out, and look at the blue sky. The moon is up, ghostlike against the deep blue. I close my eyes and feel the water move against the little canoe. The water laps quietly against the hull, and it rocks the boat slightly. I feel like I'm floating, as if the canoe and I are one and I'm suspended in a column of water, buoyant and without weight or mass.

With my eyes closed, I'm reminded of a childhood dream in

which I could fly. I feel the same now as I did in the dream, floating through space without effort. And as long as I keep my eyes closed, as long as I stay balanced on this column of water, I will continue to float, and to fly.

The Henning Tides

M y father and I were alone in a small cedar skiff, waiting for the marsh to flood. We could see the ocean break over the dunes of the barrier islands, and we could hear the violence of the open water as the offshore sandbar slowed its pace, forcing it to tumble onto the berm of the beach, white plumes of salt spray skittering across the sand.

But where we were, in a leeward marsh protected by the islands, the water was calm and silent, running in strong, deep currents through the narrow creeks that laced the salt marsh. The water rose almost imperceptibly, first covering the bases of the marsh plants, climbing slowly to the salt rim that marked the normal level of high tide, and then continuing to rise, covering the shorter grasses and obscuring the winding creeks and guts, until finally there was no marsh, but a flat expanse of building water where only patches of high grass showed. The ocean inlet between the islands, the shallow bay that separated the islands and the mainland, and the marshes were all as one, covered with water from the barrier island dunes to the line of trees on the distant mainland.

The moon was full, and the pull of the moon's gravity tugged the water toward the land. A northeast storm was offshore, and its winds pushed the ocean as the moon's gravity pulled, sending the breakers far up the beach, over the islands in low areas, and into the marshes and the forests and fields of the mainland.

I sat on a rough board bench in the bow of the skiff, holding my father's old shotgun across my lap, and I watched the tide rise, felt its silent power against the hull of the boat, which my father held steady in the current with a long oak push pole. I wondered about the tide. What if it were not to crest? What if it were to continue beyond the time of high water, and what if instead of soon ebbing, it continued to rise, even if only for a few hours? Already the marsh had been covered, the landscape erased, familiar benchmarks removed, all reference to solid land gone. The woods and fields would be next, and the houses and farms, the small towns and businesses, schools, churches. And I realized how our lives are governed by cycles such as the rising and falling of the tide, how we trust in the precision and predictability of natural events. Afloat on a flooding tide, I realize how precarious life is, how subject to sudden change, how fragile and fleeting, how dependent upon a process that has no margin for error.

It was September, and the northeast wind carried the first cold insinuations of winter. My father and I were alone. On the open water there were no other boats, none for miles. I sat in the bow of the skiff and nervously fingered the double-barreled shotgun, clicking the safety switch on and off, on and off. I felt in my pocket for the shells; I shuffled them with my hand and it made me feel warmer, shells tightly packed and heavy with

powder and lead, their brass bases clicking together in a satisfying way.

It was time, my father said. He stood and planted the long push pole into the flooded marsh, and the boat pressed forward. He told me to load the gun, and I slid in two shells and snapped it shut, checking the safety switch. My father poled the boat along the edge of a flooded salt marsh gut. Grass grows higher on the edge of a gut because it is fed by the twice-daily flush of the tides. In the flooded marsh, wisps of green grass remained above water, defining the meandering path of the guts. My father pushed the boat through these green grasstops, and I sat in the bow with the gun, watching the grass fifty yards ahead of us, looking for the bobbing heads of clapper rails, which we called marsh hens.

My father saw the first one, which was not swimming ahead of us but off to the side, attempting to flank us and get behind us. It was in the open water, bobbing and weaving, no grass in which to hide. As I lifted the gun, the rail reluctantly flushed, its wings stirring the surface of the still water. My shot peppered the water around the bird, creating an ellipse of foam. The shot seemed unnaturally loud and out of place in this marsh where the only sound was the rumble of distant waves. The marsh hen lay on its back, kicking its leg. I raised the gun to shoot again, but my father leaned forward and pressed his hand on my shoulder and I took the gun down. He pushed the boat to the bird and I picked it up, dead now, eyes glazing, wet but warm, much larger than I had expected, soft, all neck and legs, subtle browns and grays, tiny head and long bill.

My first bird. I must have been thirteen. It's a good tide, my father said, by way of congratulations.

The current had stopped flowing, and the tide crested at

seven feet above mean low water. A good marsh henning tide. We had consulted the tide table the day before, knowing that the full moon would produce a tide of about six feet above mean low. But the northeaster offshore turned a marginal henning tide into an extraordinary one.

You get these tides only a few times a year, when moon phase and weather conspire to drive the tide higher than normal, covering all but the tallest grasses of the highest marsh. The marsh hens, which normally have thousands of acres of tall grass in which to hide, become vulnerable for perhaps two hours, just before the crest of the tide and just after. So my father poled the boat along the grassy rim and I shot marsh hens, and then I poled the boat and my father shot, and as the morning grew old the sun warmed us and the tide began to fall. And as the tide fell we left the skiff and walked the high marsh, flushing rail birds from tumps of grass. By noon we filled our limits of fifteen birds each and started home.

I was wet from the waist down from walking the marsh, and as we crossed the bay and made our way back to the mainland, the wind stung. The rail birds were in a basket in the bottom of the boat, and a trickle of seawater ran from them and from my wet feet, forming a pool there. A chop was running in the bay, and as the skiff plowed into the waves, the breeze would carry the spray over me, soaking me to the skin.

My first hunting trip, a seaside baptism of full immersion, I thought, an introduction to the discomforting reality that in order for me to live, something else must die. That night our family had marsh hens for dinner. They had a wonderful wild taste, milder than wild duck, but with the flavor of the marsh: slightly salty, slightly fishlike.

I was proud of having killed these birds, of having helped feed our family. It was the directness of the process of life and death, the unbending reality of it, that made its impression upon me. My father and I went out in a flooding tide and killed food for the family, much as a hawk might, or a fox, or, for that matter, a marsh hen as it plucks a grasshopper from a blade of *Spartina* grass. I felt, in a vague and uncertain way, that I knew nature better by having participated in it, eliminating the cattle ranches, poultry farms, slaughterhouses, and grocery markets that turn the daily business of living and dying into an unseen and abstract concept. Would I have felt the same pride had I spent the day mowing my neighbors' lawns and then taken the money to the corner grocery and exchanged it for chicken or steak? Is it more moral or less moral to kill your own dinner, or to pay someone to do it for you?

In the salt marsh on that September morning, morality was not an issue, yet I knew that the violent act of ending a bird's life was heavy with implications. It was different from catching fish or clams, even though those acts also meant the death of a flounder or shellfish. Perhaps it was the violence and finality of the shot, the decision to pull the trigger, the letting of blood. It signified something, as in Isaac MacCaslin's first worthy blood in Faulkner's *The Bear:* the symbolic abandonment of childhood, a rite of passage charged with certain indelible emotions that remain with you throughout life. After many marsh henning tides, death has not become common, not without silent reverence, thankfulness, and pride—emotions I never have felt at the supermarket checkout counter.

I have come to love rail birds because they remind me that I am not above nature, but a part of it. If I destroy their marsh, they will be gone, and in the rails' absence, marsh henning tides will have no relevance, no currency, and the value of my life will be just as diminished as theirs. So the point is to protect those places that sustain rail birds, in order that a few might sustain me.

My father was my age when he first took me rail hunting. When my son is thirteen or so, I will take him rail hunting. I'll be the age my father was when he took me. Old, I thought at the time. I worried about my father as he poled the skiff. He worked in an office. What if he had a heart attack?

But my father lived to be eighty-two and died only recently. I was with him as he lay dying, and I thought not of my grief and my loss, but of marsh henning tides, of moon gravity, and of the precious, dependable cycle of ebb and flood.

My father died at 2:10 P.M. on a hot July day in a hospital emergency room. The time seems important to me. In the emergency room there was a large, white clock that, amid the clutter of very expensive medical equipment, seemed to dominate everything else. No one in the room was keeping track of the time, but time was to me the real focus.

Time is measured in precious seconds for a man with a bullet in his chest or for one severely injured in an auto accident. With each second, an injured man grows nearer to death, and it is the doctors' challenge to beat the clock, to stabilize the trauma, to reverse the inertia of dying.

For my father, there was nothing to stabilize, no life and death fight for the clock to referee. The walls of the aorta near his heart had given way, had ruptured like a worn tire, too weak to patch, too worn to function. His kidneys were failing. He lay on a narrow table, surrounded by machines that temporarily substituted for his failing body. He wore pale blue hospital pajamas, open across his white chest, which was stained with blood and antiseptics where the tubes had been inserted. The machines and the tubes held his life in suspension, not in order that the doctors could perform repairs, but so I could get there to say goodbye.

I had been on the boat, and it had been raining, so we came in early and found the message from the doctor. He used the word "grave" to describe my father's condition, but I knew even without that word that my father was approaching a moment for which he had been preparing for weeks. He had not planned his death, but he felt it coming and had given himself up to it, sometimes bitterly, but without drama and pretense.

We had not spoken of his impending death, as though if we did not acknowledge its nearness, it would go away. So, even as the clocked ticked away the seconds in the emergency room, we did not speak of death. He smiled when he saw me, and I told him he was going to be all right. There were no final messages. We both were aware of what was imminent. My father had weeks ago left his room at the retirement home where he lived and moved into the hospital wing, tired, unwilling to eat, growing astonishingly weaker and older and more resigned each day. We both knew without speaking of it what he was doing. His final gesture of reluctance came in the emergency room. "Can I go back to my room now?" he asked.

His death came without pain. Freed from the pumps and electrical circuits that prolonged both life and death, he slowly retreated. I stroked his head and wept and watched the shallowing arcs on the heart monitor.

My father was eighty-two. He had lived a rich life, chasing no wild ambitions, enjoying the simple pleasures of fishing and hunting and growing vegetables in his garden. He spent his life doing work he felt important. He served his community, loved and supported his family, and believed in God, although he did nothing at the end to invoke the supernatural. Perhaps, as in other aspects of his life, he had done that earlier, in private.

When my father had weeks earlier begun his ritual of dying, I had resented his lack of fight, his resignation. He would not eat, would not care for himself. He had always been a dapper dresser, but now he went around in soiled shirts. His socks did not match.

I talked with our family doctor and arranged various examinations, hoping for a cure to something that had no remedy. He was eighty-two. He was tired. So in the end, I too became resigned, or more accurately, accepting.

Sharing my father's death with him assuaged my grief and brought release to both of us. It brought enlightenment as well, eliminating some of the mystery and fear, the bitterness, confusion, and frustration. The despair I had earlier felt gradually gave way as I realized that what my father felt was not resignation, but metamorphosis, an inevitable modulation of body and spirit, a union of the abstract with the real.

I imagine that my father's death was much like that of his father. I have a dim image of my grandfather in his final days, his thin, white hair combed back, his white mustache neatly trimmed, his high cheekbones made more prominent by illness. He died at his home, with my father at his side, and I doubt that they spoke of death and life, or of love and grief. I'm sure my grandfather taught my father about death, just as my father taught me some forty years later. Like my father and me, they would coyly have failed to acknowledge death's presence, until it came and set them free.

I held my father's head and I watched the wall clock, and at the moment of his death the clock read ten past two. It's odd that I should remember the wall clock, so huge that it seemed surreal. But it was fitting, I think, that as I said goodbye to my father I was thinking of rail birds, of the salt marsh, and of our first hunt together.

In the flooded marsh those many years ago, with the moon's gravity coaxing the ocean onto the mainland, was my father teaching me to be a hunter? Or was he preparing me for this last day, and for one that will in time come to me? Was he, too, thinking of rail birds and marsh henning tides?

Captain John's Treasure

My great-grandfather John and his brother Thomas left their family farm in 1849 to seek their fortune in the California gold rush. Tom was twenty-two and John was sixteen.

The brothers grew up on a seaside creek that spiraled through the salt marsh and eventually spilled into Hog Island Bay, which separates Hog Island and the marshes of the mainland. When they were not tending crops, they were exploring the creeks and marshes that lay between their fields and the island beaches. Their farm was bordered by Philips Creek, a swift-running tidal creek, and they learned to handle boats not long after they learned to walk. When work on the farm was slow, they sailed out the creek to Hog Island Bay, where they caught trout and shellfish to help feed the family. And as they fished, they talked of gold.

They left in August 1849, sailing south to Panama, crossing

the isthmus by foot and horse-drawn wagon, then sailing northward again to San Francisco. John, who planned to celebrate his seventeenth birthday in California in October, became ill with yellow fever. By the time they reached San Francisco, he was near death—jaundiced, burning with fever, vomiting blood.

Cared for by his older brother, John slowly recovered, and by the following spring he had regained enough strength to set off with Tom for the California goldfields. The brothers left no record as to the amount of gold they found, but within a few years each was able to purchase oceangoing schooners and enter the shipping business, which had been their goal.

Tom formed a partnership with a man named Captain Van Falkenberg, and they began shipping goods between San Francisco and Hong Kong. Their business prospered, but in 1856 Van Falkenberg was killed when his horse and buggy overturned coming down Telegraph Hill. A year later, Tom married his late partner's widow, Jennie, and in September 1857 set out for Virginia to introduce his bride to the family.

They sailed aboard the *Sonora* to Panama, and after crossing the isthmus, boarded the *Central America*, a luxury sidewheeler and veteran of forty-three round trips between the Panamanian port of Aspinwall and New York. The *Central America* was said to have been carrying more than three tons of gold on this trip, most of which was newly minted coin destined for New York banks. Tom and Jennie, like most of the successful prospectors and businessmen returning to their East Coast families, carried a great deal of cash—more than $20,000 in uncirculated gold pieces.

Tragically, the forty-fourth trip of the *Central America* proved to be her last. On September 9 the liner encountered a vicious hurricane off the Georgia coast. Two days later her hull sprang a leak and her engine room filled with water, extinguishing the coal fires that powered her engines. Unable to make headway in the stormy seas, she floundered and went down in eighty-five hundred feet of water during the night of September 12.

Tom and Jennie stuffed their gold into a carpet bag and placed it in the captain's cabin, embraced for one final time, and she boarded a lifeboat with the other women passengers. Tom stayed with the ship and, having had experiences with typhoons in the Pacific, assisted the ship's captain first in organizing a bailing brigade and, when that failed, in helping the other passengers abandon ship.

Jennie was rescued by the brig *Marine* and taken to New York. Tom remained with Captain Herndon until the *Central America* went down, and when the liner finally went under, he climbed onto a piece of wooden decking and held on throughout the night. At dawn the bark *Ellen* patrolled the area for survivors, and Tom was found still clinging to the piece of flotsam. He was taken with other survivors to Norfolk, Virginia.

More than four hundred passengers and crew members died with the *Central America*, and Tom later told stories of wealthy forty-niners who carried to their watery graves moneybelts heavily weighted with gold. Having suffered in the California hills to collect their fortunes, they refused to relinquish them, even if it meant death.

For days, Tom and Jennie did not know of each other's fate. After arriving in Norfolk, Tom borrowed money from his family and set off for New York to search for Jennie. They eventually were reunited and returned to Virginia, finally to meet the family as husband and wife.

In one horrifying night, Tom had lost his gold rush fortune. But he and Jennie had survived the tragedy, and back in California there was still the shipping business and perhaps other fortunes to be found. So after briefly visiting the family's seaside farm, the couple set sail again for California, determined to regain the treasure that the sea had taken.

John, meanwhile, returned to Virginia, bought a ship called the *Louisiana*, and began shipping between Atlantic coast ports and the West Indies. When the Civil War began, he ran a Union blockade while returning from Puerto Rico, was chased down by the Federals along the coast of North Carolina, and was imprisoned for the duration of the war. When the war ended in 1865, he returned to his family's farm, married a local girl, and settled into a life as steward of the land overlooking Hog Island Bay.

John's parents by this time had died, and he took over the family farm, which they had named Red Bank for the bright orange clay scoured from the creek edges by the strong currents. At age thirty-two John began a pastoral second chapter of a life that had begun with more adventure than most of us will know in a lifetime. He had left home as a teenager for the California gold rush, had apparently made a great deal of money by the time he was in his early twenties, and by the time he was thirty had founded and lost a shipping business and had ended up in a Yankee prison. Although he continued to ship farm produce along the coast for a few years after the war, he seemed ready for this new life as farmer, father, and husband—a man of the land.

Perhaps John sensed all along that Red Bank farm was his calling and his fate, his ultimate mission in life, and hence his need to strike out as a teenager on a succession of Kiplingesque adventures. After the gold rush, the merchant ships, and the war, John felt free to return to the land, his wanderlust extinguished, or at least brought under control.

For more than forty years, John worked the land he had known as a boy. Yet, in what must have been a frustrating circumstance, he did not own the land. Red Bank farm had been bequeathed to Tom, the eldest son, who lived some three thousand miles away and had no inclination to return to the remote Virginia coast and coax potatoes from the sandy soil. The brothers corresponded often, and John offered many times to buy the farm, with little success.

In a letter to John dated May 25, 1869, Tom wrote to report that one of his ships, the brig *Sunny South*, had been lost in a typhoon in the China Sea. Aboard was nineteen-year-old George Martin, the brothers' nephew, who had gone to California to live with Tom and Jennie while he looked for work. In the same letter Tom again declined to sell Red Bank farm because, he wrote, "it was given me by our Father and Mother. But you can live on or use the place as you please as though it were your own free from charges for rent, and make such improvements as you wish, and if ever I come home to live I will pay you for them."

Tom, although he did not seem cut out for life as a farmer, was reluctant to sever his ties with the land, which I think represented something more to him than sandy fields, a few acres of pine woods, and salt marsh. Eventually, after numerous entreaties by John, Tom agreed to deed the land to John's sons, Thomas and John Tankard, with the stipulation that Tom retain his right to build a home on the farm should he decide someday to return to Virginia.

But Tom never did return. He remained in California, where he ran his shipping business and later an amusement park. Although he apparently succeeded in these businesses, he was often a victim of bad luck or of bad judgment. He lost several ships at sea but refused to buy insurance on vessels or cargoes.

Fire destroyed his amusement park in the 1880s, and again he had no insurance.

Ironically, one of the jobs Tom held during his periodic business reverses was that of marine surveyor for Peoples Insurance Company of San Francisco.

A San Francisco newspaper reported when Tom died in 1899 that, although he once owned vast real-estate holdings in the San Francisco area, he was near bankruptcy at the time of his death.

John, meanwhile, spent his post-Civil War years settled comfortably on the farm where he had grown up, leaving only to ship farm produce and other goods to East Coast markets. He married twice in his seventy-two years and had four sons and four daughters. His youngest daughter, my great-aunt, was born three months before John's sixtieth birthday. His second son, John Tankard, was my grandfather. The family lived in a self-contained world where the land and the sea provided for most of their needs, both physical and spiritual. In a way, the land might have served as a surrogate ship for John, a sufficient and sustainable vessel that provided all that a simple life required. Within its boundaries were the people he loved, the land and water that sustained them, and the landscape that gave him pleasure and peace.

John's affinity for his particular place on earth was deeply felt, a matter more of blood than of economics, I think, even though he depended upon the land to support his large family. His reverence for the land came from his parents, and from them he passed it to his children, and they to their children, and my father to me. And in my son, who is only six, I can already see this awakening consanguinity between person and land.

I can imagine that when Captain John was a boy, growing up

before the Civil War, he was affected by the islands and salt marshes much as I was when I was growing up. His spirit was fed by the mystery and power of the ocean, a force that was mythological, religious. His hunger was sated by fish and fowl, which the land provided in great number. His days were brightened by the warmth of winter light on slender blades of cordgrass, growing in wild meadows as far as he could see, and he was buoyed by early mornings and late evenings spent in small boats, exploring hidden coves, finding non-negotiable treasures more valuable than the yellow dust he would seek in the California hills.

He lived on a small farm of only forty or so cleared acres, but he raised enough crops to feed a family of ten and to put some money aside. They raised pigs for market and to stock the smokehouse, chickens for breakfast eggs and Sunday dinners. The family caught fish and crabs and gathered clams and oysters, and in the fall the men would shoot wildfowl. The family lived well, and when the children were grown the sons were able to buy farms of their own and the daughters were sent to college.

John's relationship with the land seems to me an ecological benchmark, something we thought we outgrew long ago but to which we once again aspire. John found beauty in the simplicity and sustainability of life on a small piece of land. All he ever needed was within his immediate line of sight, from the bay, salt marshes, and ocean to the east, to the fertile land and forests of his homeplace.

I have a handful of letters that the brothers wrote to each other over a period of about twenty-five years following the Civil War. Other than the usual inquiries as to the health of various friends and family members, Tom's letters are concerned with politics (he hated the Reconstructionists) and his topsy-turvy business interests. John seemed unconcerned with those topics, and instead dealt with family concerns, frequently prodding Tom, as tactfully as possible, to sell him the family farm.

Even in their older years, when the letters began to deal with their frequent ailments, Tom still seemed to be the adventurer, the prospector whose fortune lay just beyond the next horizon. But John seemed to be at peace with what he was and with what he had, and I can imagine his joy when Tom finally agreed to sign the farm over to John's two eldest sons.

I have no photographs of Tom as an old man, but there are several of John. It is clear he was a hard-working man. His face is deeply lined and he is lean and angular, all bone and sinew. But in all the pictures he wears a soft, unselfconscious smile. It's not the forced, vacuous grin of an old man posing for the camera, but the smile of someone at peace with the choices he has made in his life. The picture says this: While Tom spent his life searching for his fortune in California, it was John who found the treasure.

Genetic Navigation

Captain John's farmstead is gone now. All that remains of the rambling frame house are two stark, crumbling chimneys and a brick foundation wreathed in honeysuckle. The scuppernong grape vine, whose arbor framed the rear entrance of the house, has gone feral. It has smothered what remains of the rotting porch beams and is forever attempting to invade the soybean field that surrounds the house lot. Some of Captain John's fields have been replaced by pine woods; others, the low-lying ones, have been slowly claimed by an advancing salt marsh.

The land was bequeathed by my great-great-grandfather to Tom, who in turn left it to my grandfather and his brother, Captain John's first two sons. My grandfather lived on the farm, and my father was born in the east bedroom upstairs. But during my grandfather's day, farming began to change. The railroad was built in 1884, and the sailing schooners were soon made obsolete. So my grandfather left the farm and moved his family to a larger, higher, more fertile place convenient to the railroad. He still farmed the old Red Bank place, more out of habit, I suppose, than profit motive, but with the family's presence no longer on the land, it became less personal, less a daily part of their lives.

When my grandfather died in 1953, my father and uncle became owners of the land, and my uncle continued to farm it, however unprofitably. By my uncle's day, the farm had become more of an obstacle than an asset; it had become an anachronism in the corporate world of agribusiness, a helter-skelter little place of three cleared patches, some pine woods, and a salt marsh. In Captain John's day, it was sufficient to support a large family, but a century later it had become too small for efficient farming, too remote to reach with large harvesting equipment, too vulnerable to saltwater tides to sustain good yields.

My uncle, when he farmed the land, cursed the tide and kept a hopeful, helpless vigil for lethal northeast storms, which would push the seawater over the low berm of cedar and groundsel and into the fields, not a pleasant prospect for a farmer who had just put in a fall crop of corn or soybeans.

As a farmer, he never cared much for the land. Like my grandfather, he persisted from habit, or perhaps from some debt his subconscious hinted he might owe to past generations. So he held on longer than he might have, stubbornly refusing to give in to the encroaching salt marsh, the bay myrtles and sheepburrs, the capriciousness of the tides.

My father, my uncle's nonfarming partner, saw the farm from a different perspective and resisted selling. He was an accountant and worked in an office, and the farm represented an escape. He hunted his setter around the field margins and greenbrier thickets where the quail coveyed. And he liked to hike the woodlots, assessing the size and health of the pines and tracing the western property boundary from a concrete marker to a notched oak tree. My uncle had better land to farm and hunt; my father had a weekly paycheck and never had to shadowbox a northeaster.

And so, not long after my uncle retired from farming several years ago, the decision was made to sell. My father had a stroke and could no longer patrol the quail coverts, and the real-estate taxes escalated. To keep the farm would be a great luxury; to sell it would mean some degree of security for both men. The farm was sold with strict protective covenants through the Nature Conservancy and became part of its Virginia Coast Reserve, whose marshes, bays, and islands it adjoins.

It seems the story would end here, with a completed cycle of land ownership, indeed with the tragic devaluation of land, which, by corollary, implies also the cheapening of human values. But land, like people, leaves behind certain legacies that can enrich us, and in that sense, our story continues.

First there are the tangible parts of the legacy, the detritus of what we consider a time of innocence, remnants that are our link to those who came before and whose blood we share. We cling to these things tenaciously, like the old scuppernong embraces its collapsed arbor.

On a pine island where I used to hunt ducks is a small freshwater pool, a good place to see wildlife. Scrub cedars grow in thick folds around the pond, and one winter, when I was exploring the woods, I found beneath a tangled mound of greenbrier a pile of old, handmade bricks. It was here at the little pool that my ancestors dug the red clay to make the bricks that formed the foundation and fireplaces of the house.

When my wife and I built a home a few years ago, we went

down to the farm and carefully removed several hundred bricks from the grip of the honeysuckle and wild scuppernong. We carried the bricks a few at a time across a muddy field to the car, and we took them home and built a walkway at our new house. We could have bought new bricks cheaply, or we probably could have gotten some for free from other abandoned farmhouses nearer where we lived. But those bricks would have had no life.

The house had begun to collapse when I was a boy, and my father and I removed all the old heart-pine flooring and stored it in a barn, raw material for a future woodworking project. That was twenty-five years ago, and we still are searching for a project noble enough for the old wood.

Our family Christmas ritual included going to the farm to cut a cedar to decorate. So the prickly texture of cedar and the rich aroma that fills the house are part of the sensations of Christmas. Cedars are prolific at the farm, and we transplanted seedlings to our yard, where they have become special trees among the native cedars.

In glass jars I keep pottery shards collected from the bare fields of the farm. There are even a few arrow points among them. We found the old trash dump near what was once the west entrance to the farm, and we have a collection of glass jars and bottles that were my family's kitchen discards generations ago.

Beneath the old scuppernong arbor were large rocks that Captain John used as ballast stones in his sailing schooners. The rocks are now in our garden, and when we moved a few years ago, they were among the first items on the moving van.

When a piece of land, no matter how modest, has been in your family for generations, you come to know it intimately. It is as familiar as your child's voice, your lover's touch. Although I never lived on the farm, I know it. On many dark, predawn mornings in winter I have made my way without a light through the pine forest to my duck blind along the shore on the far side of the woods. Is it genetic navigation—Captain John leading me through the cedar thickets and around the mounds of greenbrier?

The pines were harvested in the thirties, when my father was a young man. The subsequent generation has grown slowly. When the stand was young, it was thick and verdant, and no one thought to thin the trees so the timber could grow taller and faster. So there are a lot of fairly old trees that look alike. But the trees that survived the harvest of the thirties are the venerable giants. They have stories to tell. My favorites are the old cedars that line the creek bank, their twisted roots laid bare by the tides. Their limbs have become contorted by storms sweeping in from the low marsh and the sea. They look painfully arthritic, but their foliage is green and lush. The roots sink deep into the clay soil and tap some ancient reservoir. These trees seem to have been here as long as the land, and their roots are so complex they seem to be part of the land. They seem not so much to bore into the soil as to embrace it, to protect and preserve it.

In our family scrapbook is a yellowed, faded photograph of my great-grandparents and their family on the porch of the old farmhouse. It is dated November 1901. Captain John wears a gray suit and vest and is standing in the center of the group. He was seventy when this photograph was taken, but he still appears lean and strong. His beard is long and untrimmed, and he holds a pipe in his left hand. His right hand is rather jauntily stuck in his pants pocket. To his left is his wife, Sue, wearing an austere black dress, her dark hair parted in the middle and pulled back tightly. Their children stand around them. The men are in suits and the women wear their Sunday dresses. Seated on the porch is Aunt Easter Badger, a former slave freed by Captain John, a woman who became, in name and in spirit, a member of the family.

I can remember only one of the persons in the photograph. The young girl seated with Aunt Easter is my great-aunt Susie, whom I saw only a few times before her death. Yet I know these people. We have the land in common, and it binds us as surely as the blood of family.

There is comfort in knowing that the land endures, that there is something about this particular piece of land that will remain with our family for generations to come. We have learned from the land, and this cycle of ownership and use, although ended, continues to offer a source for evaluation and renewal.

After the bricks have weathered back to clay and the scuppernong finally gets its revenge on the soybeans, our mark on the land will disappear. We might never have been there. But the land has left its mark on us, shaping the way we look at salt marshes, seaside bays, and barrier islands. It has taught us that humans and land are not separate, that there are cycles—the remarkable vitality of life and the inevitable transition of death—that suffuse our lives, just as there are cycles of stewardship, of fertility, of value.

Red Bank farm has made us aware and curious, has tweaked our intellect, has taught us a little about natural science, about religion, about ethics. It has made us ask questions and has sometimes given us answers. It has kept us humble.

I enjoy studying the flora and fauna of this land—the islands and marshes—because they seem familiar, like family, as if there were some supernatural affinity that might have been passed along as some sort of electrochemical charge in a link in the DNA chain.

My curiosity, indeed my awe, at how the entire system functions is probably more sensual than scientific. I enjoy the warm light of a winter sunrise on the brown shafts of *Spartina* grass as much as I enjoy knowing how *Spartina* is able to thrive in an oppressive saltwater environment that would kill less adaptable plants. I enjoy finding subtle clam sign on an exposed tidal flat, prying out the clam, and converting it to salty chowder. I like the music of a thousand greater snow geese as they rise in unison from a shallow bay at dawn, flying a mile high in lacy strings to a mainland farm field. I enjoy the grittiness of sand, the suck of mud, the startling chill and power of ocean surf as I wade in.

I am a naive observer, untrained and unrepentent of my biases. I am not a specialist; I love it all. And I have come to realize that Captain John's treasure was not a single piece of land, but an entire family of land, an ecosystem. And the most valuable part of the treasure is not the land itself, but what it has taught us.

Bibliography

What follows is a very eclectic reading list, reflecting my own interests and tastes. Some of the books are general field guides to the seashore and salt marsh, handy companions when you hike a marsh or go canoeing in a tidal creek. Others deal more specifically with the history and ecology of the Virginia barrier islands.

Several of the books listed here are out of print, but I'm listing them anyway because they contain some very good material on the islands and marshes. Many of them are available through used book dealers and are in library collections. If you're interested in the islands and marshes of the east coast, they're worth searching out.

Obviously, there are many more books on salt marsh ecology than I have space to list here, and there are field guides on everything from shorebirds to seashells. This is sort of a personal reading list, a collection of material I've found valuable for one reason or another.

Badger, Curtis, and Rick Kellam. *The Barrier Islands.* Stackpole, 1989. A history of the Virginia barrier islands, including approximately three hundred old photographs of barrier island villages, hunt clubs, people, and more.

Bailey, Harold H. *The Birds of Virginia.* J. P. Bell Company, 1913. An interesting look at the status of birds in Virginia at the turn of the century. Especially good treatment of plovers, skimmers, terns, and other birds that nest on the islands. Out of print, but available in rare and used book shops.

Carson, Rachel. *The Sea Around Us.* Signet, 1950. Classic text on the ocean.

Carson, Rachel. *The Edge of the Sea.* Signet, 1955. A fascinating look at the intertidal zone.

Connett, Eugene, ed. *Duck Shooting along the Atlantic Tidewater.* Bonanza, 1947. Chapter on Eastern Shore hunting and decoys.

Dixon, Thomas. *The Life Worth Living.* Doubleday, 1905. Dixon, a popular preacher, lawyer, novelist, and lecturer in the late 1800s and early 1900s, lived for a few years on the Virginia coast and near Gloucester, Virginia. The book includes some hunting and fishing stories dealing with the barrier islands, as well as several photos. Out of print but available.

Gosner, Kenneth L. *Altantic Seashore.* Houghton-Mifflin, 1978. A Peterson Field Guide, and a good companion on a beach hike. Crabs, shells, worms, grasses—all in one pocket-sized book.

Hunter, Alexander. *The Huntsman in the South*. Neale Publishing Company, 1908. A classic look at waterfowl hunting in the post-Civil War years. Several chapters on Hog and Cobb islands, as well as the Carolina coast, the Dismal Swamp, and fox hunting. Out of print and scarce.

Kaufman, Wallace, and Orrin H. Pilkey, Jr. *The Beaches Are Moving—The Drowning of America's Shoreline*. Duke University, 1983. A good text for anyone interested in beach dynamics and island migration. Read this before you build that beach house.

Lippson, Alice Jane, and Robert L. Lippson. *Life in the Chesapeake Bay*. Johns Hopkins Press, 1984. A good description of life on the tidal flats, beaches, and shallow tidal waters of the Chesapeake. Most of the information applies to the Atlantic seashore as well.

Meanley, Brooke. *The Marsh Hen*. Tidewater Publishers, 1985. Nice little book on the clapper rail, by a professional biologist.

Reiger, George. *Wanderer on My Native Shore*. Simon and Schuster, 1983. An outstanding collection of essays on the Atlantic coast by one of America's best contemporary conservation writers.

Shiras, George. *Hunting Wildlife with Camera and Flashlight*. 2 vols. National Geographic, 1935. Two chapters on Revel's Island, where Shiras kept a cottage, complete with photographic darkroom. Nice photos circa 1890 of shorebirds coming to decoys. The book went through many printings and is fairly easy to find.

Silberhorn, Gene M. *Tidal Wetland Plants of Virginia*. Virginia Institute of Marine Science, 1976. Good book on marsh plants, ranging from saltwater plants, such as *Spartina* and *Salicornia*, to the rushes and grasses of brackish and freshwater wetlands. Nice illustrations by Mary Warinner.

Teal, John, and Mildred Teal. *Life and Death of the Salt Marsh*. Random House, 1969. A wonderful discussion of *Spartina* and other salt marsh plants. Readily available in paperback.

Terres, John K., ed. *Discovery: Great Moments in the Lives of Outstanding Naturalists*. Lippincott, 1961. Includes a chapter on Cobb Island by ornithologist Olin Sewall Pettingill, who took his bride to the island for their honeymoon in 1933. Out of print but available.

Terres, John K. *The Audubon Society Encyclopedia of North American Birds*. Knopf, 1987. A monumental work and a must for all amateur ornithologists. Seven pounds worth of information about birds.

Turman, Nora Miller. *The Eastern Shore of Virginia*. Eastern Shore News, 1964. A good basic history of the Eastern Shore.

Warner, William W. *Beautiful Swimmers*. Atlantic Monthly Press, 1976. Wonderful account of the blue crab.

Whitelaw, Ralph T. *Virginia's Eastern Shore*. Virginia Historical Society, 1951. The definitive, two-volume history of homes and landholdings on the Eastern Shore. Modern reprints available.

134